John Cottingham is Professor of Philosophy at the University of Reading, and co-editor and translator of the standard English edition of *The Philosophical Writings of Descartes*. He has written numerous books and articles, and his many publications on early modern philosophy include *Descartes*, *The Rationalists*, *Philosophy and the Good Life*, and the *Cambridge Companion to Descartes*.

HOW TO READ

HOW
TO
READ

DESCARTES

JOHN COTTINGHAM

Granta Publications, 12 Addison Avenue, London W11 4QR

First published in Great Britain by Granta Books, 2008

A CIP catalogue record for this book is
available from the British Library.

1 3 5 7 9 10 8 6 4 2

ISBN 978 1 84708 004 2

Typeset by M Rules

Printed and bound in Great Britain
by CPI Bookmarque, Croydon

CONTENTS

SERIES EDITOR'S FOREWORD

How am I to read *How to Read*?

This series is based on a very simple, but novel idea. Most beginners' guides to great thinkers and writers offer either potted biographies or condensed summaries of their major works, or perhaps even both. *How to Read*, by contrast, brings the reader face-to-face with the writing itself in the company of an expert guide. Its starting point is that in order to get close to what a writer is all about, you have to get close to the words they actually use and be shown how to read those words.

Every book in the series is in a way a masterclass in reading. Each author has selected ten or so short extracts from a writer's work and looks at them in detail as a way of revealing their central ideas and thereby opening doors on to a whole world of thought. Sometimes these extracts are arranged chronologically to give a sense of a thinker's development over time, sometimes not. The books are not merely compilations of a thinker's most famous passages, their 'greatest hits', but rather they offer a series of clues or keys that will enable readers to go on and make discoveries of their own. In addition to the texts and readings, each book provides a short biographical chronology and suggestions for further reading, Internet resources, and so on. The books in the *How to Read* series don't claim to tell you all you need to know about Freud, Nietzsche and Darwin, or indeed Shakespeare and the Marquis de Sade, but they do offer the best starting point for further exploration.

Unlike the available second-hand versions of the minds that have shaped our intellectual, cultural, religious, political and scientific landscape, *How to Read* offers a refreshing set of first-hand encounters with those minds. Our hope is that these books will, by turn, instruct, intrigue, embolden, encourage and delight.

Simon Critchley
New School for Social Research, New York

ABBREVIATIONS

The sources of the extracts from Descartes's writings that appear at the start of each chapter are identified in each case by the following standard abbreviations:

'**AT**' refers (by volume and page number, e.g. 'V 34') to the definitive Franco-Latin edition of Descartes by C. Adam & P. Tannery, *Œuvres de Descartes*, 12 vols, rev. edn., Paris: Vrin/CNRS, 1964–76;

'**CSM**' refers (by volume and page number, e.g. 'II 45') to the English translation by J. Cottingham, R. Stoothoff and D. Murdoch, *The Philosophical Writings of Descartes,* vols I and II. Cambridge: Cambridge University Press, 1985; and

'**CSMK**' refers (by page number) to *The Philosophical Writings of Descartes*, vol. III, *The Correspondence*, by the same translators plus A. Kenny. Cambridge: Cambridge University Press, 1991.

INTRODUCTION

Of all the great canonical philosophers in the western tradition, few have such an ambivalent reputation as René Descartes. On the one hand he is revered as the 'father of modern philosophy', and his best-known works serve as standard introductory texts for countless philosophy students. On the other hand, his doctrines, on the nature of the mind and its relation to the body, on the foundations of knowledge, and on the methodology of science, are regularly condemned by philosophers today as the source of many damaging confusions and errors. The extracts chosen for this volume are designed to indicate how Descartes influenced the development of subsequent western thought, to reveal why his ideas have aroused such hostility in recent times, and to bring out those aspects of Descartes's vision of knowledge and reality that may still have something important to say to us today.

Descartes's ideas burst forth on the European intellectual scene in the middle decades of the seventeenth century, and were soon generating enormous interest. His first work, the *Discourse on the Method*, appeared anonymously in French in 1637, but not long afterwards in 1641, his masterpiece, the *Meditations*, came out in Latin – still at that time the international language of the learned world – thereby ensuring a wide audience. Three years later, Descartes published (again in Latin) a large and comprehensive account of his entire philosophical system, in four parts. This was the *Principles of Philosophy* (*Principia philosophiae*), which not only outlined the metaphysical foundations of Descartes's new ideas, but also provided a complete system of physics, explaining a wide range of phenomena, from stars and planets and comets to tides, magnets, earthquakes, fires, and a great deal else, right down to detailed explanations of such things as the production of glass. This was a complete scientific system; and its beauty was that it aimed to explain all the diverse phenomena of the universe, celestial as well as terrestrial, using only a few simple mathematical covering laws. Together with those of his great contemporary, Galileo, Descartes's ideas in effect heralded the birth of modern science.

Descartes was reacting against the 'scholastic' philosophy of his predecessors. Scholasticism, the system of thought that dominated philosophy for much of the Middle Ages and Renaissance, was founded by Aquinas in the thirteenth century, and in turn it owed much to the philosophy of Aristotle (fourth century BC). In its accounts of the natural world, it relied very largely on qualitative explanations. The world consisted of a large number of different substances, each with its own essential qualities or forms: earthly matter moved downwards because of its quality of 'heaviness'; the nature of fiery matter was to move upwards; and so on. The job of the philosopher was to classify the various natural kinds of substance, according to their essential definitions.

Descartes realized that such descriptions did not have any real explanatory or predictive power. What was needed was an approach which focused not on quality, but on *quantity*. In place of scholasticism's multiplicity of 'substantial forms' and 'real qualities', Descartes saw the entire universe as composed of a single, homogeneous material stuff, which he called 'extended substance' (in Latin, *res extensa*); this was divided up into particles whose behaviour could be explained entirely in terms of mathematical variables specifying size, shape and motion. This represented an enormous gain in simplicity and in precision. As Descartes proudly declared in his *Principles of Philosophy*, 'I recognize no matter in corporeal things apart from that which the geometers call quantity, i.e. that to which every kind of division, shape and motion is applicable' (see Chapter 1). Only a decade after Descartes's early death (in 1650), the young Dutch-Jewish philosopher Benedict Spinoza was publishing an enthusiastic exposition of Descartes's *Principles*, and he was but one of many influential thinkers who were captivated by the 'new philosophy' – the new mathematical conception of science. The actual equations and ratios produced by Descartes we can now see to be flawed (they were soon to be superseded by the work of Isaac Newton, later in the seventeenth century), but his general quantitative approach to physics remains one of the cornerstones of our modern scientific worldview.

There was, however, one crucial exception to Descartes's complete mathematical schema for explaining reality, and this was *consciousness*. Matter was extended (in three dimensions), divisible, and therefore subject to mathematical analysis; mind, by contrast, Descartes saw as entirely different: a mind did not occupy space, but was an *un*extended and therefore indivisible substance. So in addition to the vast, unified, extended material substance that was the subject of physics, there were also an indefinite number of individual conscious substances – minds or souls. These formed a kind of separate domain, outside the realm of physics, not scientifically explicable, and indeed wholly immaterial. Such was the celebrated division of reality now known as 'Cartesian dualism' ('Cartesian' being derived from 'Cartesius', the Latin version of Descartes's name): mind and matter were utterly distinct and separate kinds of thing. And from this it followed that each one of us, considered as a conscious, thinking being, is wholly distinct from the body. As Descartes put it in his *Discourse on the Method*, 'This "I", that is to say the soul, by which I am what I am, is entirely distinct from the body, and would not fail to be what it is even if the body did not exist.'

Cartesian dualism, though it probably corresponds to how a lot of people still think about mind versus matter, bequeathed enormous problems to philosophy. Is a human being really an immaterial spirit mysteriously inhabiting the physical mechanism of the body – a 'ghost in the machine', as the twentieth-century British philosopher Gilbert Ryle scathingly put it? Descartes's successor Spinoza, impressed as he was by Descartes's general programme for physics, could not stomach his account of the mind, and homed in on the puzzle of how a supposedly immaterial substance could possibly interact with a material body: were we to suppose that some purely mental 'act of will' had the power to move around bits of the brain or nervous system?

Descartes was himself very concerned to allow for the fact that a human being was, as he put it, an 'essential unity', not a mere amalgam of the incompatible elements of mind and body. 'I am not merely *lodged* in my body as a sailor in a ship, but very closely joined and as it were *intermingled* with it,' he wrote in the *Meditations*. He insisted that our sensations and emotions (hunger, thirst, anger, fear, etc.) were by their very nature such as to involve elements of *both* mind and body, and were signs that we were not pure incorporeal beings but genuine creatures of flesh and blood. Modern philosophy has made a variety of attempts to solve, or even to dissolve away, the complex problem of the relationship between the mental and the physical; but despite the strong reaction against Descartes's views in our own time, the shape of much subsequent debate on the nature of the mind still bears recognizable traces of Descartes's legacy.

Although Descartes was one of the inaugurators of the modern age, much of his worldview preserved strong links with the ideas of his medieval and Renaissance predecessors. One striking instance of this concerns the role of God in his philosophy. In addition to the two categories of substance already mentioned (mind and matter), Descartes insists on the primacy of an utterly independent, uncreated substance – God. God discharges a crucial function in Descartes's system as the 'creator and preserver' who sustains the entire universe, and keeps it in being in accordance with immutable laws. The very possibility of the new mathematical science rests, for Descartes, on the eternal and unalterable decrees of God. What is more, since matter is, in

Descartes's system, wholly inert, defined simply by the property of being extended, there would be no motion or activity whatsoever in the universe without the dynamic power of God to generate and conserve its movement.

In human terms, God is also vital in Descartes's system as the guarantor of objective knowledge. One of Descartes's main aims was to set new standards for knowledge and science by sweeping away the often obscure and ill-defined notions of his predecessors, and insisting on a foundation of 'clear and distinct' ideas. The mechanism for weeding out obscurity and prejudice is his famous methodical doubt, which enables us to discard any beliefs that are not absolutely certain. The universal application of doubt initially discloses one bedrock certainty – one undeniable truth that survives the onslaught of doubt: this is the celebrated 'I am thinking, therefore I exist' (*Cogito, ergo sum*). But this would remain an isolated and meagre item of individual subjective awareness unless the inquiring mind could reach beyond itself to something more stable and constant – the eternal being who created us and endowed us with the power of knowledge. Hence God is for Descartes a vitally necessary object of discovery for the human inquirer in his search for truth.

Descartes holds that the human mind, though finite, is in a sense a partial mirror of the divine mind. So while there are many things we limited creatures do not know, it is vital for Descartes's system of knowledge that the things we *do* know clearly and distinctly are true. God would be a deceiver if he allowed us to go wrong in the fundamental intuitions of the intellect (for example, our grasp of the basic truths of logic and mathematics). Here again we see the importance of God for Descartes: the divine creator is not merely an optional extra, or a separated item of 'faith' that does not connect with the rest of philosophy or science; on the contrary, God's existence, and his goodness, are the basis of all we can know. Here, despite the 'modernity' of Descartes in other respects, we see an aspect that puts a gulf between his worldview and the bleaker, increasingly secularized outlook of our own times. For many modern thinkers, we humans are essentially 'on our own', without any guarantees, or any eternal underwriter to establish the objectivity of our claims to knowledge; many, indeed, would say that science consists in no more than tentative conjectures, which will always be open to revision. For Descartes, things are very much more secure: what he called the 'light of reason' is a divine gift imparted to our human minds, which offers us the hope of discerning the true nature of reality.

Anyone who believes in a perfect and benevolent creator, as Descartes does, must have some responsibility to explain how it is that we so often go astray. For although we may be endowed with the divine light of reason, it is an undeniable fact that humans often fall into error. Traditional philosophical accounts of moral error (or sin) had, from the time of St Augustine onwards, explained it as stemming from our own free will or choice. Descartes's strategy in the case of intellectual or scientific error is similar. Our intellect being finite, but our will infinite, error arises through our misuse of the will: instead of restricting our beliefs to what we clearly and distinctly perceive, we rashly jump in and give our assent when the truth is not clear. Descartes here offers an interesting perspective on the perennial philosophical problem of free will. To be able to exercise free choice is a blessing, but also a potential curse, since it can lead us astray when we act with insufficient knowledge. True freedom, the highest grade of freedom, Descartes implies, is something rather more restricted – namely, deliberately confining ourselves to areas where the truth is totally clear. And when we do focus on items which have such transparent clarity, then we will spontaneously assent to the truth: 'from a great light in the intellect follows a great inclination of the will'.

We now seem to be involved in a subtle shift from questions about science and knowledge to areas (like freedom, choice, error, and sin) that impinge on moral philosophy. This is no accident; for Descartes, unlike many of today's narrowly specialized practitioners of the subject, saw philosophy as a unified system, embracing all areas of human endeavour – including not just abstract and theoretical concerns, but the human condition and the conduct of life. The whole of philosophy, he wrote in the 1647 preface to the French edition of his *Principles*, is like a tree, of which metaphysics are the roots, physics the trunk, and particular disciplines, including medicine and morals, the branches.

Human life, for Descartes, is in one respect fundamentally unlike animal life – our use of reason and language sets us apart. In our post-Darwinian world, we are very much aware of the links between ourselves and the other animals with whom we share the planet, and Descartes's strong separation between the human and the animal domains has generated much criticism. Since he regarded animals as essentially part of the physical world, he thought their behaviour could be explained just like any other part of 'extended stuff', in terms of the size, shape and motion of the particles of which they are composed. This has given rise to the view that Descartes regarded animals as mere machines – mechanical automata; but as we shall see, Descartes's position is rather more nuanced than is often supposed, and his legacy in this respect needs to be interpreted with care.

As regards the good life for human beings, the study of which remained one of the goals of his philosophy, Descartes became preoccupied in his later years with the ancient problem of the management of the 'passions' (feelings and emotions) – those dark and often recalcitrant aspects of our nature that sometimes risk blowing our lives off course and making us act irrationally. Descartes's programme for the training of the passions prefigures many modern approaches in harnessing the results of science (including physiology and psychology) in order to allow us to develop better patterns of living, and improve the quality of our lives.

Descartes is a Janus-faced figure, with revolutionary ideas that point forwards towards our modern age, while often implicitly looking backwards towards the earlier culture that he inherited.

That ambivalence is part of his fascination. His thinking continues to interact with our own: there is much that we feel like
challenging, yet much we can recognize as still having something
to teach us. Above all, his unified vision of philosophy, bringing
together the theoretical and the practical, the scientific and the
moral, the theme of our dependence on God and the theme of
our independent search for truth – all this makes him one of the
richest and most rewarding of philosophers to study. As the rep-
resentative extracts included in this book should demonstrate, he
is a supremely clear writer, one who resolutely avoids defensive
jargon in favour of speaking directly to the ordinary person of
'good sense' – that quality which he declared to be 'the most
widely distributed in the world'. One of the very greatest
thinkers of all time, he encourages each of us to accompany him
on an enthralling journey towards knowledge and understanding.
We may not, nor would he have expected us to, agree with all he
says; but with him as our guide we will surely be able to grasp a
great deal of what philosophy is about, and what makes it
supremely worth doing.

THE NEW SCIENCE

Good sense is the best distributed thing in the world: for everyone thinks himself so well endowed with it that even those who are the hardest to please in everything else do not usually desire more of it than they possess. In this it is unlikely that everyone is mistaken. It indicates rather that the power of judging well and of distinguishing the true from the false – which is what we properly call 'good sense' or 'reason' – is naturally equal in all men . . .

Those long chains composed of very simple and easy reasonings, which geometers customarily use to arrive at their most difficult demonstrations, had given me occasion to suppose that all the things which can fall under human knowledge are interconnected in the same way. I thought that, provided we refrain from accepting anything as true which is not, and always keep to the order required for deducing one thing from another, there can be nothing too remote to be reached in the end or too well hidden to be discovered. I had no great difficulty in deciding which things to begin with, for I knew already that it must be with the simplest and most easily known. Reflecting, too, that of all those who have hitherto sought after truth in the sciences, mathematicians alone have been able to find any demonstrations – that is to say, certain and evident reasonings – I had no doubt that I should begin with the very things that they studied. From this, however, the only advantage I hoped to gain was to accustom my mind to nourish itself on truths and not to be satisfied with bad reasoning. Nor did I have any intention of trying to learn all the special sciences commonly called 'mathematics'. For I saw that, despite the diversity of their objects, they agree in considering nothing but the various relations or proportions that hold between these objects. And so I thought it best to examine only such proportions in general, supposing them to hold only between such items as would help me to know them more easily . . .

But I must admit that the power of nature is so ample and so vast, and these principles so simple and so general, that I noticed hardly any particular effect of which I do not know at once that it can be deduced from the principles in many different ways – and my greatest difficulty is usually to discover in which of these ways it depends on them. I know no other means to discover this than by seeking further observations whose outcomes vary according to which of these ways provides the correct explanation.

Discourse on the Method *[Discours de la méthode, 1637]*
Extracts from Part I, Part II and Part VI (AT VI 1, 19, 64–5:
CSM I 111, 120–1, 144)

The only principles which I accept or require in physics are those of geometry and pure mathematics; these principles explain all natural phenomena, and enable us to provide quite certain demonstrations regarding them. I will not here add anything about shapes or about the countless different kinds of motions that can be derived from the infinite variety of different shapes. I am assuming that my readers know the basic elements of geometry already, or have sufficient mental aptitude to understand mathematical demonstrations. For I freely acknowledge that I recognize no matter in corporeal things apart from that which the geometers call quality, and take as the object of their demonstrations, i.e. that to which every kind of division, shape and motion is applicable. Moreover, my consideration of such matter involves absolutely nothing apart from these divisions, shapes and motions; and even with regard to these, I will admit as true only what has been

deduced from indubitable common notions so evidently that it is
fit to be considered as a mathematical demonstration.

Principles of Philosophy [Principia philosophiae, 1644]
Extract from Part II, article 64 (AT VIIIA 78–9: CSM I 247)

Descartes is a multi-faceted thinker, and there are many ways
into his system of thought. This opening chapter deals with the
public face: the scientific and methodological programme that
launched his career, and for which he was best known in his own
time. One could equally approach Descartes by looking at the
more personal and individual dimension of his quest for knowledge, as discussed in Chapter 2, which traces the dramatic
journey of the meditator from doubt towards certainty. But
whether you start with the scientific edifice or its metaphysical
foundations, you will sooner or later be confronted with an inte-
grated system.

'Philosophy' in Descartes's time was a comprehensive term
which included not just the topics dealt with by present-day academic philosophers, but also the whole of what is now called
natural science; indeed, Descartes probably saw his explanatory
theories of natural phenomena as among his most important
philosophical achievements. He had great confidence that his
specific theories were accurate; but irrespective of the details, he
was convinced that he had arrived at a new and spectacularly
improved general framework or methodology for scientific
inquiry. The set of extracts above provides the key elements of
the new Cartesian method in science.

Descartes's first published work, which appeared anonymously
in French in 1637, is called *Discourse on the Method*; its full title is
*Discourse on the method of rightly conducting one's reason and reaching
the truth in the sciences*. 'Reason' did not, for Descartes, imply any
special technical training or elaborate learning; on the contrary,
as the first extract (from the opening of *Discourse*) indicates, he
regarded it as linked to 'good sense' – the 'most equally distributed things in the world'. Elsewhere, he speaks of a 'natural

light', present in all human beings, and he insists that this can take us much further than abstruse erudition and elaborate book learning. Sceptical about much of the traditional classical education he had received himself, he thought the supposed 'wisdom' of past ages was often a mere collection of prejudices or preconceived opinions – an obstacle to knowledge rather than its embodiment.

Mathematics, for the young Descartes, provided something completely different from the morass of preconceived opinions and vague probabilities that often passes for knowledge. In paragraph two of the extract, he speaks of the 'long chains of reasonings' found in geometry as paradigms of reliability and clarity. In standard Euclidian geometry (as set out in the *Elements* of Euclid, dating from the third century BC) one starts from self-evident principles or 'axioms', and each proposition or theorem is then demonstrated as following from those axioms in a set of absolutely clear steps, so that it is logically linked to what has gone before through a process of reasoning that aims to be completely watertight – what is called 'deductive' reasoning. The premises are ones that are supposed to be irresistibly and transparently true, and the conclusions follow so rigorously that they cannot be denied, on pain of contradiction. This kind of clarity, reliability and deductive rigour is what Descartes aims for in his new science.

Geometry is of course concerned with shapes or 'figures', such as circles and triangles, so one may ask if Descartes was proposing that all of science should be 'geometrical' in this strict and narrow sense. Much of his work in physics did indeed focus on size and shape. It aimed to show how all the complex phenomena we observe around us could be explained in terms of the interactions of particles of matter at the micro level; and these interactions were to be explained purely in terms of the size and shape and motion of the particles in question.

So geometry is vitally important. But as the extract makes clear, Descartes does not make a fetish of geometry for its own sake. Geometry attracts him because it deals with the 'relations or proportions that hold between objects'; in other words, it helps us to see formal mathematical patterns and ratios that underlie all phenomena. Along with the *Discourse*, Descartes published three scientific essays as illustrations of his new method: *Optics*, *Meteorology* and *Geometry*; the method in all three of these apparently diverse subjects involved applying abstract principles of mathematical ratio or proportion to the particular problems in each area. Thus, the *Optics* formulates, with tolerable accuracy, what we now know as the mathematical laws of refraction of light, while the *Geometry* was partly concerned with abstract algebraic relations that underlie arithmetical and geometrical studies, thus uniting the study of shape and of number. What Descartes is concerned with, in short, is a universal template for scientific knowledge – what he sometimes called *mathesis universalis* ('universal mathematics' or 'the universal discipline'). As he put it in his early unpublished study, *Rules for the Direction of our Native Intelligence* (*c*.1628), 'I came to see that the exclusive concern of mathematics is with questions of order or measure, and that it is irrelevant whether the measure in question involves numbers, shapes, stars, sounds, or any other object whatever. This made me realise that there must be a general science which explains all the points that can be raised concerning order and measure, irrespective of the subject matter' (AT X 278: CSM I 19).

It was an inspiring vision. In place of the plethora of separate subjects that had characterized the scholastic system of his predecessors, each with their separate methods and standards of precision, and each describing essentially different kinds of phenomena, Descartes was proposing a *universal key* – the study of a formal, rationally determinable structure underlying the whole cosmos. Like Galileo, who some twenty years earlier had declared that the 'great book of the universe' was written in mathematics, Descartes was aspiring to discover the ultimate code that would unlock the secrets of nature.

The mathematical model of knowledge, alluring though it

may be, can nevertheless be a misleading one, unless it is interpreted with care. As noted above, the classical geometrical system of Euclid was a strictly 'deductive' one – that is to say, all the propositions in the system were rigorously deduced from self-evident starting points. The kind of knowledge involved in such a system is known by philosophers as 'a priori' knowledge – that is to say, it operates completely independently of experience. You can do Euclidian geometry from the armchair, working only from the given definitions and rules. You may perhaps need a pencil and paper to help you if your mathematical imagination is not too good, but you certainly don't need to go round measuring lines or squares. Geometry is not an experimental science.

This may make us wonder about the ambitious claim contained in the final extract quoted above, from Descartes's *Principles of Philosophy*. The general methodology is clear enough, from what we have already seen: quantity, ratio, proportion, size and shape – these are the building blocks of the new science. But what about the resounding final sentence – 'I will admit as true only what has been deduced from indubitable common notions so evidently that it is fit to be considered as a mathematical demonstration'? Can the scientist really aspire to unravel all the secrets of the universe a priori (independently of experience) – from the armchair, as it were? And can scientific reasoning really match this mathematical template of rigid deductive proof?

Descartes is perhaps over-egging the cake here. For centuries, following the lead of Aristotle and then Aquinas, knowledge (*episteme* in Greek, or in Latin *scientia*) had been taken to involve rigid deductive demonstration from self-evident axioms; in promoting his new scientific system, Descartes certainly did not want to present it as falling short of this hallowed ideal. Nevertheless, if we look at the details of his system, and how his explanations are worked out in practice, his actual conception of science is by no means as rigid as the deductive model might suggest. The passage from Part Six of the *Discourse* (the third paragraph of our opening extract) makes this point quite straightforwardly. Descartes frankly admits that the power of nature is so vast, and his own mathematical principles so simple and so general, that it is not possible in practice to deduce each effect from the principles in a rigorous manner.

Instead, Descartes acknowledges the need for observations. The picture seems to be that the scientist begins with an abstract schema of explanation, but when descending to the particular explanation of magnetism, say, or the formation of glass, or the behaviour of the tides, it is necessary to introduce auxiliary hypotheses, which are tested against experience or observation. The precise way in which nature works, among the many possibilities consistent with the first principles, has to be settled by 'seeking further observations whose outcomes vary according to which of these ways provides the correct explanation'.

This recourse to – indeed, insistence on – the role of observation in science brings Descartes much closer to what we now think of as modern scientific methodology. The point is an important one, since it is still common in textbooks to hear Descartes described as a 'rationalist', as opposed to an 'empiricist'. (The former term comes from the Latin *ratio*, meaning 'reason'; the latter from the Greek *empeiria*, 'experience'.) According to this venerable classification, philosophers are divided into those, on the one hand, who believe in the power of reason to generate knowledge purely a priori, independently of experience, and, on the other hand, those who think all knowledge must come from observation or experience, via the five senses. Descartes certainly believed in an innate 'natural light' of reason, and he certainly thought that a great deal of knowledge could be established a priori; furthermore (as we shall see in the next chapter), he warned that the deliverances of the senses could often be doubtful and confusing. So in these respects he may be thought of as belonging to the 'rationalist' tradition which goes right back to Plato. On the other hand, as the passage under discussion from the *Discourse* clearly shows, he did not aim to spin out the entirety of science using only abstract reasoning from the armchair. His scientific writings are full of diagrams and descriptions of observations. While not, perhaps, a great experimenter in the modern sense, he was fully aware that his abstract mathematical principles needed to be supplemented by hypothesis and observation in order to be brought to bear on the real world around us.

This last point brings us to a final important aspect of Descartes's 'geometrical' approach to science. The mathematical study of size and shape is a distinctly abstract affair. It is also a distinctly static affair. However elegant the equations which Descartes introduces in order to describe the particles of 'extended matter' of which his universe is composed, there does not on the face of it appear to be any explanation of *movement*, let alone dynamic notions such as force or resistance, which started to play a serious role in Newtonian mechanics not long after Descartes's death. The explanation of the actual workings of the physical universe cannot, it seems, come from pure mathematics alone.

Descartes's answer, as so often in his system, was to be found in God. 'God is the primary cause of motion,' he observes elsewhere, and 'he always preserves the same quantity of motion in the universe' (*Principles*, Part II, article 36). So the transition from knowledge of pure mathematics to knowledge of the real physical cosmos requires us to acknowledge a dynamic power or force that supports the whole material world. This is not something inherent in matter; for matter, in Descartes's system, is simply 'extended stuff', geometrically shaped particles of a certain breadth, depth and height. Instead, it is an external, transcendent power, a divine power that is responsible for all existence and all motion, a power that (as Descartes often acknowledges) exceeds our power to comprehend it fully.

This may seem to take us worlds away from modern science. It could not be further from the spectacular modern insight, due to Einstein, that matter and energy are interchangeable, or, to put it another way, that power is inherent to matter, not something imposed on it from outside. But it is worth remembering that Einstein's famous predecessor, Isaac Newton, concurred with Descartes in maintaining that the explanations of mathematical physics are incomplete without a divine creator and conserver. At all events, the 'mathematicization of science', which Descartes proclaims in our opening extracts from the *Discourse* and the *Principles*, undeniably points the way forward to the modern world. From Descartes onwards, the path of science was to be inextricably bound up with a quantitative, mathematical understanding of the universe.

2

DOUBT AND CERTAINTY

Some years ago I was struck by the large number of falsehoods that I had accepted as true in my childhood, and by the highly doubtful nature of the whole edifice that I had subsequently based on them. I realized that it was necessary, once in the course of my life, to demolish everything completely and start again right from the foundations if I wanted to establish anything at all in the sciences that was stable and likely to last . . .

Whatever I have up till now accepted as most true I have acquired either from the senses or through the senses. But from time to time I have found that the senses deceive, and it is prudent never to trust completely those who have deceived us even once.

Yet although the senses occasionally deceive us with respect to objects which are very small or in the distance, there are many other beliefs about which doubt is quite impossible, even though they are derived from the senses – for example, that I am here, sitting by the fire, wearing a winter dressing-gown holding this piece of paper in my hands, and so on. Again, how could it be denied that these hands or this whole body are mine? Unless perhaps I were to liken myself to madmen, whose brains are so damaged by the persistent vapours of melancholia that they firmly maintain they are kings when they are paupers, or say they are dressed in purple when they are naked, or that their heads are made of earthenware, or that they are pumpkins, or made of glass. But such people are insane, and I would be thought equally mad if I took anything from them as a model for myself.

A brilliant piece of reasoning! As if I were not a man who sleeps at night, and regularly has all the same experiences while asleep as madmen do when awake – indeed sometimes even more improbable ones. How often, asleep at night, am I convinced of just such familiar events – that I am here in my dressing-gown, sitting by the fire – when in fact I am lying undressed in bed! Yet at the moment my eyes are certainly wide awake when I look at this piece of paper; I shake my head and it is not asleep; as I stretch out and feel my hand I do so deliberately, and I know what I am doing. All this would not happen with such distinctness to someone asleep. Indeed! As if I did not remember other occasions when I have been tricked by exactly similar thoughts while asleep! As I think about this more carefully, I see plainly that there are never any sure signs by means of which being awake can be distinguished from being asleep. The result is that I begin to feel dazed, and this very feeling only reinforces the notion that I may be asleep . . .

[Yet] whether I am awake or asleep, two and three added together are five, and a square has not more than four sides. It seems impossible that such transparent truths should incur any suspicion of being false. And yet . . . since I sometimes believe that others sometimes go astray in cases where they think they have the most perfect knowledge, how do I know that God has not brought it about I too go wrong every time I add two and three or count the sides of a square, or in some even simpler manner if that is imaginable?

Meditations on First Philosophy [Meditationes de prima philosophia, 1641]
Extracts from First Meditation (AT VII 17–21: CSM II 12–14)

Descartes saw his mission in life as that of sweeping away the rubble of preconceived opinion and constructing a new system of knowledge based on 'clear and distinct' principles. In the extract above we see perhaps his most famous presentation of how the rubble was to be cleared away in the opening of his philosophical masterpiece, the *Meditations*, published in Latin in 1641.

Descartes's 'meditator', travelling along a lonely and isolated path which each reader is expected to follow, decides to 'demolish everything' and 'start again right from the foundations'. The demolition weapon to be used is *doubt*. He begins by doubting the evidence of the five senses: they have often proved unreliable, and it is prudent not to trust those who have deceived us even once. Then the doubt becomes fiercer. Worries about the reliability of the senses can hardly call into question such absolutely basic beliefs as that I am sitting here by the fire, wearing a winter dressing gown. But wait! Have I not sometimes vividly *dreamed* such things, only to find upon waking that I am really in bed?

Some people find the 'dreaming argument' (as it has come to be known) rather silly; others (perhaps those who have experienced vivid dreams that seemed utterly real at the time) find it disturbing and convincing. Descartes's aim in deploying the argument is to soften us up, to undermine our usual complacency, by asking us to consider how much of what we are confident about can really be said to amount to knowledge. To the solitary mind of the meditator, it begins to seem as if nothing is certain – perhaps there is really no world 'out there' but only the images of dreams.

The difference between vivid dreamers and those who remember their dreams (if at all) merely as a vague blur is a fascinating one. Recent research has established that a significant number of people are 'lucid' dreamers – that is, they have totally vivid and coherent dream experiences, which may even include such thoughts as, 'This all seems very strange – I think I must be dreaming!' or, 'This is dreadful, I wish I could wake up!' If you have had such experiences, you may well be disposed to take

Descartes's argument seriously. Others will be unimpressed, and may ask if it even makes sense to wonder whether one is awake; or they may suggest that even if it does make sense, you could always perform some test to settle the matter – perhaps you can pinch yourself, and if it hurts this will tell you for sure you that are not asleep. But actually, of course, it is not that simple; for lucid dreamers are quite capable of thinking, *in their dream*, such thoughts as, 'I had better check whether I am awake.' They may even dream they are pinching themselves, and that it hurts, and conclude they are awake. Recent dream research has produced reports of many who have experienced 'false awakenings' – the experience of seeming to wake up from a dream, only to find that the 'waking up' was simply another part of the dream. A significant number of people have even experienced such nightmares prolonged into a whole series of 'false awakenings', each carrying the seeming reassurance that this time one must *surely* be awake, until something strange about the experience makes the hapless sleeper realize that it is after all just a continuation of the dream.

Descartes himself was in the habit of 'lying in' and dozing late into the morning (when lucid dreams are particularly common) – a habit he had retained since childhood, when because of his poor health he was given permission to get up late at his boarding school. It seems certain that he himself was a lucid dreamer. Indeed, his early notebooks refer to a particularly vivid and troubling series of dreams which he had as a young man while travelling in Southern Germany in 1619 (a journey explicitly referred to in Part I of the *Discourse on the Method*). He had spent the day meditating in a stuffy, 'stove-heated room' (*poêle*), and went to bed filled with mental excitement, believing he had discovered the foundations of a new system of knowledge. Three successive dreams followed. In the first he was assailed by phantoms, and felt a violent wind which made it hard for him to walk upright. He sought refuge in the chapel in a college quadrangle (this part of the dream no doubt incorporated memories of the College of La

Flèche, near Poitiers, where he had spent most of his boyhood). A friend approached him and spoke of someone who had a present for him 'which he imagined was a melon brought from some foreign country'. The second dream involved a loud and violent noise, and flashes of light. The third, calmer dream featured two books, the first a dictionary or encyclopedia which he took to represent 'all the sciences collected together', while the second was a volume of poetry containing the Latin verse *Quod vitae sectabor iter?* ('What road in life shall I follow?'). The story is told by Descartes's early biographer, Adrien Baillet, in his account of the life of Descartes published in 1691, and is based on material from Descartes's own diaries.

Descartes clearly believed these dreams were of enormous significance, and took them to signal his destiny as the founder of a new philosophical system. But what is striking is the detail and vividness of the dreams, and the point (reported by Baillet) that 'being in doubt as to whether what he had just seen was a dream or a vision, not only did he decide while still asleep that it was a dream but he even speculated on the interpretation before waking up'.

The discussion of dreaming in the *Meditations* is thus not a mere 'academic' exercise, but something that had strong personal resonances in Descartes's own experience. Dreaming for Descartes did indeed involve entry into a coherent, if strange and imaginary, world, where the normal, external correlates of one's mental experience cannot be taken for granted. 'I see clearly,' says Descartes in the extract from the *Meditations*, 'that there are no certain marks by which being awake can be distinguished from being asleep.' The whole line of thought is disorientating and disturbing, and itself produces a kind of mental vertigo – and Descartes notes that this very feeling of being dazed only reinforces the notion that one may be asleep.

True to his faith in mathematics (see Chapter 1), Descartes thought that even the supposition that I am dreaming cannot undermine mathematical certainty: 'Whether I am awake or asleep,' he goes on to observe in our passage, 'two and three added together make five, and a square has no more than four sides.' But then a more sinister, and even more radical, doubt begins to surface. Could not God, who is after all supposed to be all-powerful, bring it about that I go wrong every time I count the sides of a square or add two and three? Or even more radically (the meditator goes on to speculate shortly after the quoted passage), perhaps there is no God at all. We should remember that even raising this as a theoretical possibility was still highly risky in the seventeenth century, but Descartes is resolute in following the thread of his argument. If there were no God, then our minds, instead of being divinely bestowed on us, must have evolved by mere chance or some random chain of imperfect causes; and in that case there would be even less reason to trust our mental powers of mathematical reasoning. Either way, God or no God, there seems no guarantee that I can trust even my most basic rational intuitions, such as the belief that two and three make five.

This is the high-water mark of Cartesian doubt. And towards the end of the First Meditation, Descartes sums things up by bringing in the dramatic device of a 'malicious demon', bent on systematic deception:

> I will suppose that not God, who is supremely good and the source of truth, but rather some malicious demon of the utmost power and cunning has employed all his energies in order to deceive me. I shall think that the sky, the air, the earth, colours, shapes, sounds and all external things are merely the delusions of dreams which he has devised to ensnare my judgement. (AT VII 22: CSM II 15)

It is an early version of the kind of radically disorientating scenario that has become familiar in our own time, from such successful science-fiction movies as *The Matrix* (written and directed by Andy and Larry Wachowski in 1999). The whole of 'reality' – or what we take to be reality – may be a series of deceptive impressions somehow implanted in our minds by some malign and alien power.

Is there any way out? Philosophers since classical times had agonized over various moves and counter-moves in the long-running debate between 'sceptics' and their opponents, and Descartes's contemporary, the English philosopher Thomas Hobbes, complained that he should have chosen to serve up this 'ancient material'. (Hobbes was in Paris when the *Meditations* were published, having fled from the English civil war, and he was shown a draft of the work, and invited by Descartes's editor, Marin Mersenne, to comment on the manuscript. His 'Objections', together with those of other prominent philosophers, were included, with Descartes's 'Replies', in the first edition of 1641.)

Hobbes's jibe is in fact a bit unfair; nothing quite like the malicious demon had ever been suggested in ancient Greek or Roman discussions of scepticism. But one might nevertheless feel that elaborate sceptical scenarios of this kind are too artificial, too exaggerated, to carry real conviction. In the century following Descartes, the brilliant Scottish philosopher David Hume was aptly to remark:

> The great subverter of . . . the excessive principles of scepticism is action, and employment, and the occupations of common life. These [sceptical] principles may flourish and triumph in the schools, where it is, indeed, difficult, if not impossible, to refute them. But as soon as they leave the shade, and by the presence of the real objects, which actuate our passions and sentiments, are put in opposition to the more powerful principles of our nature, they vanish like smoke, and leave the most determined sceptic in the same condition as other mortals. (*An Enquiry concerning Human Understanding* [1748], Section XII)

Human nature, Hume reminds us, will always win, in the end, over philosophical argument. You may be excited for a while by

'Matrix' scenarios, but when you put on the kettle for a cup of tea, or (to use Hume's example) relax over a game of backgammon, you will find the wild doubts fading into the distance. Descartes himself would probably have agreed. He himself described his sceptical reasonings in the First Meditation as 'hyperbolical', and remarked in the *Synopsis* printed at the start of the *Meditations* that 'no sane man' has ever doubted the existence of the ordinary world around us.

Nevertheless, the arguments have an important point. They serve to remind us, in the first place, that the senses are not always reliable; in the second place, that the vividness and subjective convincingness of an experience is no guarantee that the events it depicts are actually occurring; and third, that even an apparently utterly simple judgement such as 'two plus three makes five' presupposes the reliability of our mental faculties – something we cannot take for granted. Descartes was not himself a sceptic, but was interested in seeing how far doubt could be pushed. His doubt was a weapon designed to challenge entrenched 'preconceived opinions' or 'prejudices' (in Latin *praejudicia* – literally, 'pre-judgements') (AT VII 22: CSM II 15).

In exploring how our firmest convictions might be mistaken, Descartes may have had at the back of his mind the recent devastating discovery that the Earth itself – firm and immovable though the Bible had declared it to be – was in fact spinning on its axis every twenty-four hours, and also revolving annually around the Sun. Nicolaus Copernicus had first proposed the quite literally Earth-shaking suggestion of a Sun-centred planetary system forty years before Descartes's birth; and Descartes's contemporary Galileo Galilei had begun to amass observational support for it while Descartes was a schoolboy. Some twenty years later, Galileo was condemned by the Inquisition for advancing the heliocentric hypothesis just when Descartes, who himself supported the sun-centred picture, was just about to publish his own account of the physical universe. The whole of the seventeenth century was indeed a time of genuine doubt and insecurity about the nature of the cosmos, and the spirit of the times was aptly heralded by the English poet John Donne in his long elegy 'An Anatomy of the World', written in 1611, while Descartes was still in his teens:

> [The] new Philosophy calls all in doubt,
> the element of fire is quite put out;
> the Sun is lost, and th' Earth, and no man's wit
> can well direct him where to look for it.

Descartes, destined to become one of the chief promoters of the 'new philosophy', was impatient to clear away the rubble of previous confusion and error, and this explains the primary focus of his inquiries, announced in the very subtitle of the First Meditation: 'What can be called into doubt'. But his purpose was not doubt for its own sake. His plan was to use the tool of doubt to establish a new bedrock of certainty. We shall see in the following chapter where he found it.

3

CONSCIOUSNESS AND SELF-AWARENESS

So serious are the doubts into which I have been thrown as a result of yesterday's meditation that I can neither put them out of my mind nor see any way of resolving them. It feels as if I have fallen unexpectedly into a deep whirlpool which tumbles me around so that I can neither stand on the bottom nor swim up to the top. Nevertheless I will make an effort and once more attempt the same path which I started on yesterday. Anything which admits of the slightest doubt I will set aside just as if I had found it to be wholly false; and I will proceed in this way until I recognize something certain, or, if nothing else, until I at least recognize for certain that there is no certainty. Archimedes used to demand just one firm and immovable point in order to shift the entire Earth; so I too can hope for great things if I manage to find just one thing, however slight, that is certain and unshakeable.

I will suppose that everything I see is spurious. I will believe that my memory tells me lies and that none of the things that it reports ever happened. I have no senses. Body, shape, extension, movement and place are chimeras. So what remains true? Perhaps just the one fact that nothing is certain.

Yet apart from everything I have just listed, how do I know that there is not something else which does not allow even the slightest occasion for doubt? Is there not a God, or whatever I may call him, who puts into me the thoughts I am now having? But why do

I think this, since I myself may perhaps be the author of these thoughts? In that case am not I, at least, something? But I have just said that I have no senses and no body. This is the sticking point: what follows from this? Am I not so bound up with a body and with senses that I cannot exist without them? But I have convinced myself that there is absolutely nothing in the world, no sky, no earth, no minds, no bodies. Does it not follow that I too do not exist? No: if I convinced myself of something, then I certainly existed. But there is a deceiver of supreme power and cunning who is deliberately and constantly deceiving me. In that case I too undoubtedly exist, if he is deceiving me; and let him deceive me as much as he can, he will never bring it about that I am nothing so long as I think that I am something. So after considering everything very thoroughly, I must finally conclude that this proposition, *I am, I exist,* is necessarily true whenever it is put forward by me or conceived in my mind.

Meditations on First Philosophy *[*Meditationes de prima philosophia,

1641]

Extracts from Second Meditation (AT VII 23–5: CSM II 16–17)

The First Meditation is a dark night of the soul. Everything is doubted, and I am left in a state of acute anxiety. My cosy array of previously accepted beliefs have turned out to be open to question, and this leaves me longing for my lost security. I would be happy to slide back into those comforting old opinions; indeed, Descartes writes at the close of the Meditation, 'I dread being shaken out of them, for fear that my peaceful sleep may be followed by hard labour when I wake, and that I have shall have to toil not in the light, but in the inextricable darkness of the problems I have now raised.'

Yet it is worth following Descartes along his lonely path of extreme doubt. He wrote the *Meditations* not as an abstract treatise in philosophical theory but (as the name implies) as a set of exercises to be performed by each of us. As he warned in the book's preface, 'I would not urge anyone to read this book except those who are able and willing to meditate seriously along with me, and to *withdraw their minds from the senses*.' In raising the issue of withdrawal from the senses he was invoking an ancient tradition. Plato argued in the fifth century BC that the philosopher, to gain true enlightenment, must struggle out of the 'cave' – the world of our ordinary beliefs based on the changing and unreliable data of the senses – and take the hard path upwards to the brighter, lighter world of the pure intellect. Much later, St Augustine, writing during the collapse of the Roman Empire at the turn of the fourth century AD, followed Plato in mistrusting the senses: we need to escape from the tossing ocean of sensory inputs and find a more stable foothold on the solid shore of reason.

The old Platonic and Augustinian metaphors recur in Descartes. Darkness needs to be replaced by daylight; the watery chaos of the whirlpool by at least one firm and solid place to stand. But where to find a foothold, if everything is uncertain? How to find secure ground if we have rejected the five senses, the very apparatus that seems to be the basis of anything we can know? Descartes quotes another source from classical Greece, Archimedes, one of the great mathematicians and engineers of the ancient world. Famous for his studies of the fulcrum, Archimedes is reported to have said, 'Give me a place on which to stand, and I will move the whole Earth!' So Descartes does not ask for a whole body of knowledge, just for a single point of certainty which can get him started.

So, once again, let us follow Descartes on his solitary journey. You are quite alone. You cannot trust your senses. You may be dreaming. Indeed your whole life, in some strange way, may be a dream: everything that comes into your head (if indeed you have a physical head at all!) may be part of an illusion systematically implanted into your consciousness by the malicious demon, or his modern equivalents, the manipulators of the Matrix. In short, you are totally and utterly deceived about everything.

But wait: if you are deceived, surely you must at least exist.

Augustine, who got there before Descartes, put it as follows: *si fallor, sum* ('if I am deceived, I exist'). There is after all *something* that cannot be doubted. As Descartes puts it in our passage: 'let him deceive me as much as he can, he will never bring it about that I am nothing so long as I think I am something'. Total doubt is self-refuting; for the very act of doubting establishes the existence of the doubter as something that cannot be doubted.

We are now moving towards Descartes's famous first principle. As he expressed it in Part Four of his earlier work, the *Discourse*: 'I noticed that while I was trying to think that everything was false, it was necessary that I who was thinking this, was something. And observing that this truth, *I am thinking, therefore I exist* [*je pense, donc je suis*], was so firm and sure that all the most extravagant suppositions of the sceptics were incapable of shaking it, I decided that I could accept it without scruple as the first principle of the philosophy I was seeking.' In the *Principles of Philosophy* (*Principia philosophiae*), published seven years later in 1644, the famous French phrase *je pense, donc je suis* appears in its even more famous Latin equivalent, *Cogito, ergo sum*. Perhaps the most celebrated dictum in all of western philosophy, this simple, self-evident proposition emerges as the first secure foothold – the 'Archimedian point' – of Descartes's system of knowledge.

If we are to read Descartes accurately, we need to notice several things about his famous dictum. First of all, it is a pronouncement in the *first person singular*: it has to be formulated with the word 'I' (or its equivalent in French or Latin or whatever language), rather than with the word 'you', or 'he', or even 'we'. 'You think, therefore you exist' will not quite do. After all, I may not be sure whether *you* are thinking, and even if you stand in front of me and assure me that you do, it seems possible that you might be a figment of my imagination, or part of a dream. This reinforces the point made earlier that Descartes expected each reader to 'meditate seriously along with him'. Everyone needs to do the meditation for himself or herself. By pushing doubt to the limit, each individual doubter will be brought face to face with his or her indubitable existence – the existence of the subject who is actually now thinking, or who is engaged in the process of trying to doubt everything.

Second, and connected, the validity of 'the Cogito' (as Descartes's dictum has come to be called) is not something to be demonstrated on a blackboard, as it were, like some impersonal truth, such as 'two plus two makes four'. It is a directly personal item of awareness that is apprehended in the very individual act or performance of doubting it. It is not really a conclusion that is inferred or derived from a set of premises, or even from a single premise. Some commentators have called it a *performance* rather than an inference. It is something you have to *do*, in order fully to appreciate how it works.

Third, it is not a timeless truth, but one whose assurance is very temporary. There is nothing necessary about my existence. I (and the same goes for you) might cease to exist at any time. The demon, or 'deceiver of supreme power and cunning' imagined by Descartes, would find it easy, on the assumption that he is extremely powerful as well as malicious, to terminate me whenever he chooses. And even without bringing in such extravagant scenarios as that of the malicious demon, we all know only too well that our existence is finite and contingent: we depend from moment to moment on a host of sustaining causes (oxygen, nutriment, gravity, atmospheric pressure, temperature), any one of which, were it to fail or change substantially, would lead to our immediate extinction. So there is nothing very secure or guaranteed about the truth of the proposition *sum* ('I exist'). The same goes, it seems, for the proposition *cogito* – 'I think': the activity of thinking could cease at any time. So where *is* the certainty of the Cogito?

Only in this: that so long as I *am* thinking, there is nothing that can happen, *during that time*, to make me not exist. Hence in our extract Descartes makes the *temporary* or (as the philosophers of language put it) *temporally indexed* character of the Cogito very clear: '*I am, I exist*, is necessarily true *whenever it is put forward by me or conceived in my mind.*' A few paragraphs after our quoted passage he makes the point even more explicitly: 'I am, I exist, that is certain. But for how long? For as long as I am thinking.'

The thin and temporary nature of the Cogito may make one think it is too insubstantial to allow any real conclusions to be derived from it. Some activity certainly now seems to be going on, some conscious process that cannot be doubted as long as it continues. But that is all. It is not even clear that I am entitled to say anything very much about the 'I' that is doing the thinking. If, for example, the 'I' is supposed to refer to some particular Englishman who was born in the twentieth century, or to a seventeenth-century French philosopher who is meditating in his study chewing his quill pen, then this would involve a whole barrage of further assumptions, which seem very far from certain. After all, Descartes has just asked us to suspend all our previous beliefs and suppose that there is 'no external world, no sky, no earth'; he can hardly now blithely re-import his 'preconceived opinion' that he is a certain type of human animal, with a head and arms and legs, or assume that he is sitting by the fire in his winter dressing gown (the scenario described in the First Meditation). All this, he has been at pains to tell us, might be an illusion.

Descartes is quite straightforward and above board about all this. Having established that he exists, he immediately proceeds (in the paragraph following our extract) to sound a warning note: 'But I do not yet have a sufficient understanding of what this "I" is that now necessarily exists, so I must be on my guard against carelessly taking something else to be this "I", and so making a mistake in the very item of knowledge that I maintain is the most certain and evident of all.' There are really two inquiries, not one, that Descartes sets himself in this part of the Second Meditation. The first is to establish whether there is not something he knows for certain, despite the most extreme application of doubt. And he answers that in the affirmative, with his first principle, *Cogito, ergo sum*: whatever else may be doubted, I know that as long as I am thinking, I must exist. The second question, which is much more difficult, is to establish what this 'I' refers to. Having established *that* I am, the task now is to settle *what* I am.

Here Descartes is on much shakier ground. For the normal, common-sense answer to the question 'What am I?' would seem to be something like 'A human being'. And a human being is, as we all know, a certain type of warm-blooded creature, a featherless biped, with arms and legs and so on. The precise biological details may perhaps (at a stretch) be thought of as problematic, but at the very least the term 'I' surely here refers to someone with a *body* (as opposed to, say, a spirit or a ghost). After all, we normally think of ourselves as *located* somewhere in a pretty robust, bodily sense. I am sitting *in the garden*; I am typing *at my desk*; I am *drinking a cup of green tea*.

For Descartes, however, all these physical references take us way beyond what we are strictly entitled to say about ourselves. 'At present,' he goes on in the Second Meditation, 'I am not admitting anything except what is necessarily true. I am, then, in the strict sense *only* a thing that thinks; that is, I am a mind, or intelligence, or intellect or reason . . . But for all that, I am a thing which is real and which truly exists. But what kind of thing? As I have just said, a *thinking thing*.' So having established quite straightforwardly *that* he is, Descartes is now advancing a far more controversial thesis about *what* he is – namely, that he is simply a 'thinking thing'. His earlier formulation, in the *Discourse on the Method*, brings out the point in all its starkness:

Next [having established *that* I exist], I examined attentively *what* I was. I saw that while I could pretend that I had no body and that there was no world and no place for me to be in, I could not for all that pretend that I did not exist . . . From this I knew that I was a substance whose *whole essence or nature is simply to think*, and which does not require any place or depend on any material thing, in order to exist. Accordingly this 'I' – that is the soul by which I am what I am – is entirely distinct from the body, and indeed is easier to know than the body, and would not fail to be whatever it is, even if the body did not exist. (AT VI 32–3: CSM I 127, emphasis added)

If you are prepared to go along with Descartes here, notice what you are conceding. You are agreeing, in effect, to the proposition that you are some kind of *purely mental entity*. The key phrase is: 'this "I"' (*ce Moi*), that is to say the soul by which I am what I am'. Very many people do of course believe that each of us has a unique soul, and that the essential nature of each person, their true self, consists in just this. So Descartes's position is by no means idiosyncratic or outlandish. But his logic, at least, does seem questionable. In the passage in the *Discourse* just quoted, he seems to rest the argument on his ability to *suppose* that he has no body: if I can imagine myself without a body, then body cannot be part of the essential 'me'. As it stands, this reasoning is, unfortunately, flawed. I can imagine my cat without its DNA; but does that show that the DNA in question is not essential to the identity of my cat? The answer seems to be: No; all it shows is that I don't know very much about biology. If I am ignorant of genetics, I can imagine all sorts of things about how identity could be preserved in the absence of a particular DNA structure, but my imaginings cut no ice when it comes to what is essential to making something what it is.

This parallel argument is only an analogy, but it seems to show that Descartes's ability to 'pretend' or imagine that he can exist without the body does not succeed in showing that the true self, what makes him *him*, could really exist in the absence of a body. His answer to the question '*What* am I?' – namely, 'Merely a thing that thinks' – seems to be arrived at in a way that is seriously flawed.

It is worth asking what has led Descartes to this position. One answer, offered by many philosophers nowadays, would be that he has already distorted his perspective by supposing that he can establish a foundation of certainty on the basis of individual, private meditation. 'I am here quite alone,' Descartes says at the start of the *Meditations*; and he proposes to tear down the edifice of existing belief and build up a new and reliable one from scratch – all on his own, as it were. The perspective of Cartesian inquiry, it is often said, is an essentially *private* one; and it is no accident that the first principle that emerges from this perspective is a *first-personal* truth, the Cogito: *I* think, therefore *I* exist. And the privacy is now reduced further, to an essentially subjective mind, a private centre of consciousness, a 'thinking thing' and nothing else.

The twentieth-century philosopher Ludwig Wittgenstein famously attacked the idea that a private, first-personal perspective could be the basis for any satisfactory account of knowledge. He implicitly attacks Descartes for making the defective assumption that thought and language could operate at all in a wholly private, first-personal domain. Language, Wittgenstein argues (in his *Philosophical Investigations*, 1953), is necessarily a matter of public rules for the correct application of terms. And if meaning requires public, socially determined rules, then the whole Cartesian procedure of radical doubt turns out to be confused. For even in expressing or mentally formulating the doubt, I am, inevitably, making use of language and concepts; and this already presupposes the very existence of the 'external' world, and of a public community of human language-users, all of which I am officially supposed to be doubting.

Some of the implications of Wittgenstein's attack on the idea of 'private language' are still being debated by philosophers. But as far as Descartes's own procedure in the *Meditations* is concerned, it seems questionable whether his perspective is quite as 'private' and isolated as is so often alleged by the modern critics. It is true that he adopts a solitary or 'solipsistic' perspective in order to focus his thoughts; and having doubted all other existing things, he is left (perhaps not surprisingly) only with his own conscious self as the sole indubitable starting point. Yet in spite of this he does, as we shall see, implicitly recognize severe constraints on his thinking – constraints which come from a source other than himself. The more he examines himself, the more he realizes that there are certain aspects of reality he is not in charge of, including the whole domain of ideas, which determine his thinking in accordance with certain rules, whether he likes it or not. The source of this 'public' or objective structure constraining his thinking turns out to be rather different from that proposed by the followers of Wittgenstein. It is not just a function of the linguistic conventions of society, but depends on something much more powerful – namely, the supreme power of God. To the role of God in Descartes's system we shall now turn.

4

GOD

Next, reflecting on the fact that I was doubting and that consequently my being was not wholly perfect (for I saw clearly that it is a greater perfection to know than to doubt), I decided to inquire into the source of my ability to think of something more perfect than I was; and I recognized very clearly that this had to come from some nature that was in fact more perfect than me.

Regarding the thoughts I had of many other things outside me, like the heavens, the earth, light, heat and numerous other things, I had no such difficulty in knowing where they came from. For I observed nothing in them that seemed to make them superior to me; and so I could believe that, if they were true, they depended on my nature insofar as it has any perfection, and, if they were not true, I got them from nothing, in other words, they were in me because I had some defect. But the same could not hold for the idea of a being more perfect than my own. For it was manifestly impossible for me to get this from nothing; and I could not have got it from myself, since it is no less contradictory that the more perfect should result from the less perfect, and depend on it, than that something should proceed from nothing.

So there remained only the possibility that the idea had been put into me by a nature truly more perfect than I was, and even possessing in itself all the perfections of which I could have any idea, that is – to explain myself in one word – by God.

> To this I added that, since I knew of some perfections that I did not possess, I was not the only being which existed . . . but there had of necessity to be some other, more perfect being on which I depended and from which I had acquired all that I possessed. For if I had existed alone and independently of every other being, so that I had got from myself what little of the perfect being I participated in, then for the same reasons I could have got from myself everything I knew I lacked, and thus been myself infinite, eternal, immutable, omniscient, omnipotent; in short I could have had all the perfections which I could observe to be in God.
>
> Discourse on the Method [Discours de la méthode, *1637*]
> *Extract from Part IV (AT VI 33–5: CSM I 128)*

Descartes's arguments concerning God are often glossed over as an embarrassing piece of cultural baggage that his philosophy would be better off without. In fact God is absolutely central to Descartes's philosophical system, as first seen in Descartes's scientific programme. It now emerges with even greater force in the metaphysical foundations of his system. The modern inclination to try to 'secularize' Descartes's thought shows more about the prejudices of our own time than it reveals about how to interpret Descartes correctly. Despite the widespread current tendency to view Descartes as if he were a modern 'analytic' philosopher, interested only in language or 'epistemology' (the theory of knowledge), the whole tone and thrust of our extract reveals his links to an earlier contemplative tradition whose values need to be understood properly before they are summarily discarded.

One of Descartes's medieval predecessors, the Franciscan friar Bonaventure, asked in his widely admired *Journey of the mind towards God* [*Itinerarium mentis in Deum*, 1259], 'How would the intellect know that it was a defective and incomplete being, if it had no awareness of a being free from every defect?' Descartes, in our extract, follows a similar path. Having reached awareness of himself as a thinking being, he starts to reflect on what he knows of himself, and is immediately brought up against the stark fact of his own imperfection. The mere truth that he is ignorant of so many things, the mere condition of doubt and uncertainty in which he finds himself, and his lack of any immediate power to remedy these defects – all these things show that his nature is imperfect.

That very recognition of our imperfection (a premise we can hardly deny to Descartes) seems to presuppose the idea of some standard of perfection of which we fall short. As Descartes puts it in the Third Meditation, in language strikingly similar to Bonaventure's, 'How could I understand that I doubted, or desired – that is, lacked something – and that I was not wholly perfect, unless there were in me some idea of a more perfect being which enabled me to recognize my own defects by comparison?'

For Descartes, the next step in the argument is to ask how I got this idea of perfection. Could I have constructed it from my own resources? Many of my ideas seem to come from a source external to myself, such as the ideas of ordinary phenomena around me like stones and trees and heat and light; and the natural inference is that the phenomena in question themselves produced the ideas in me. Yet a sceptic could say that I dreamed them up, constructing them by using simply my own mental powers of imagination. Painters and poets weave ideas together using their creative intelligence, so who is to say that my ideas of the objects around me may not have their source in nothing more than myself? Well, you may or may not think this plausible in the case of stones and trees and so on; but there is one idea, Descartes reasons, which we just *couldn't* have produced by our own powers. The idea of *perfection*, of a perfect being, could not have been dreamt up by me alone (or by anyone like me), since, as we have seen, *I am imperfect*; and as Descartes insists in our extract, *the more perfect cannot come from the less perfect*.

Suppose you found a mentally defective patient producing a

highly complex mathematical proof – the kind of proof it would take a doctorate in mathematics to understand. Or suppose you found an utterly illiterate patient of subnormal IQ producing an intricate and highly intelligent novel like Jane Austen's *Pride and Prejudice*. In both these cases you would surely conclude: the patient could not have produced these ideas from his own resources – he must have got them from someone else, or copied them out from a book. In the words of the ancient axiom formulated by the classical Greek philosopher Parmenides (and widely known in the Middle Ages in its Latin version, *ex nihilo nihil fit*), 'nothing can arise out of nothing'. The ideas involved in the complex mathematical proof or the intricate novel cannot just have come from nowhere. What this suggests is a kind of 'causal adequacy principle': *the cause must be adequate to the effect.* Our patient (the cause) was just not adequate to produce the effect (the mathematical proof or the novel); his unfortunate defects, his imperfections, are the best possible evidence that he could not have devised these ideas himself.

Descartes's reasoning is really as simple as this, and it does have a certain elegance and plausibility. Here is how he develops it in the Third Meditation, having surveyed all the ideas he finds within his mind, and then decided that in most cases there is no reason why he should not have been able to construct them all by himself:

> There remains only the idea of God; and I must consider whether there is anything in the idea which could not have originated in myself. By the word 'God' I understand a substance that is infinite, eternal, immutable, independent, supremely intelligent, supremely powerful, and which created both myself and everything else (if anything else there be) that exists. All these attributes are such that, the more carefully I concentrate on them, the less possible it seems that they could have originated from me alone. So from what has been said it must be concluded that God necessarily exists. (AT VII 45: CSM II 31)

Yet intuitively plausible as this reasoning is, there is a serious weak point – namely, the 'causal adequacy' principle we have just been discussing. Why should not the more perfect come from the less perfect? Did not life (a complex and intricate phenomenon) originate from less perfect causes (inorganic molecules)? Did not highly advanced life forms originate from more primitive life forms? The success of Darwinian explanations of evolution, via the elementary mechanisms of random mutation and natural 'selection' (a simple function of variations in success in the struggle for survival), has made our contemporary worldview far less ready to accept the axiom on which Descartes relies, that 'the more perfect cannot result from the less perfect'.

Nevertheless, there is something striking about our human mentality, which perhaps does call for some special explanation. We are clearly finite creatures, limited, lacking, imperfect in all sorts of ways. We are utterly *contingent* beings – that is to say, wholly dependent on a host of conditions without which we could not exist. And yet despite that contingency, despite that finitude, we clearly have within us the idea of infinity. Man is a being who, in the words of Descartes's compatriot and contemporary Blaise Pascal, 'infinitely transcends himself'; there is something in us that reaches beyond our finite situation and our contingent limitations towards that which is eternal and unlimited. Of course, all this shows is that we have the *idea* of infinite perfection, not that there is any real being who matches that idea. But the mere desire, the mere reaching forward towards the transcendent, is perhaps something that cannot entirely be dismissed. The Augustinian tradition, which clearly influenced Descartes (though he makes no explicit reference to it in his published writings), had identified the *restlessness* of the human spirit as a sign of its unavoidable quest for the divine. 'You have made us for yourself,' cries Augustine in his *Confessions* (*c*.AD 397), 'and our heart is restless until it finds repose in you!' For the believer, the very *idea* of God, its presence within our minds as a hope, as an aspiration, as a sign of all that we lack, is at least some kind of basis for supposing that our hope is not in vain.

This may seem to take us beyond philosophy to the realm of religious faith; and to that extent it exceeds the bounds of Descartes's method of argument, which aims to be strictly rational and logical. Although Descartes did on occasion refer to the 'supernatural light' of faith as a privileged source of knowledge, he clearly wanted his philosophy to be based on what he called the *lumen naturale* – the 'natural light' of reason. Nevertheless, there remains something very Augustinian in the way Descartes takes the interior path of meditation, and searches within himself in order to find God. 'Go not outside,' Augustine had declared in his treatise *On True Religion* (*De vera religione*, AD 391), 'but return within thyself; in the inward man dwelleth the truth.' And Descartes implicitly concurs with this, in his summary at the end of the Third Meditation:

> It is no surprise that God, in creating me, should have placed this idea [of himself] within me, to be, as it were, the mark of the craftsman stamped on his work . . . The mere fact that God created me is a very strong basis for believing that I am somehow made in his image and likeness, and that I perceive that likeness, which includes the idea of God, by the same faculty which enables me to perceive myself.

The theocentric character of Descartes's system is thus apparent right from the start of his reconstruction of human knowledge. The very first discovery, after the discovery of the indubitability of the thinking self, is the discovery of God. Almost every student of philosophy knows of Descartes's *Cogito, ergo sum* ('I am thinking, therefore I exist'); far fewer are aware of the striking formula he produced in one of his earliest works, *Sum, ergo Deus est*: 'I exist, therefore God exists' (AT X 422: CSM I 46).

But is Descartes's approach really 'theocentric'? The Catholic

Church, of which Descartes was all his life a member, has long been suspicious of Cartesian philosophy, regarding it as unorthodox and potentially subversive of the faith. Soon after his death, Descartes's writings were placed on the Church's *Index* of prohibited books; and in the succeeding centuries the image of Descartes as an anti-clerical, anti-religious force has proved strangely resilient, even though it conflicts with virtually everything we know of his actual character and work.

In his *Memory and Identity*, reflecting on the decline of moral values in the twentieth century, the late Pope John Paul II traced the philosophical roots of the decline to the ideas of Descartes. The trouble started, he argued, with the way Descartes constructed his philosophy, basing it on the foundation of individual self-awareness: instead of starting (as St Thomas Aquinas had in the thirteenth century) with Divine Self-subsistent Being, Descartes in his famous Cogito argument had given primacy to each person's individual consciousness, so that philosophy thereafter had become concerned with what is contained within the ambit of subjectivity, rather than with the reality that is independent of it.

But the charge is misplaced. Although Descartes begins with his own self-awareness, the primacy of the Cogito is simply an *epistemic* priority – a priority in what he called the 'order of discovery'. If I try to doubt everything, the first thing I find I cannot doubt is my own existence; but Descartes was nonetheless clear that such self-awareness leads directly to awareness of God. *Sum, ergo Deus est*: I am, therefore God exists. In knowing myself I immediately recognize my complete dependence on a power infinitely greater than myself. *Epistemically*, in terms of the individual's quest for knowledge, I may come first; but *ontologically*, in the order of reality, God retains, for Descartes, absolute primacy.

The close of the Third Meditation sees the meditator speaking in unmistakably religious tones. 'Let me here rest for a while in the contemplation of God himself and gaze upon, wonder at, and adore the beauty of this immense light.' The meditator's voice here is the voice of the worshipper (or perhaps of the philosopher in the Platonic sense that implies a genuine love or yearning), rather than of the detached analytic philosopher. Or maybe it would be better to say that Descartes is adopting a modality of thought found in the writings of many of the early Christian fathers, where analytic philosophizing and religious contemplation are inextricably intertwined. The tone and impetus of the meditating is less one of critical scrutiny than one of humble submission. Just as for Augustine no salvation was possible without the gift of divine grace, so the scientific truth that Descartes seeks is dependent from the start on the 'immense light', mirrored in each individual soul, or (to revert to Descartes's earlier metaphor) the idea of God being stamped there like the 'mark the craftsman has set on his work'.

These aspects of Descartes's thinking may not be congenial to our modern, highly secularized conception of philosophical inquiry, but if we suppress them we blind ourselves to the true character of his work. And if we are prepared, at least for a while, to lay down our secular prejudices, we may, by looking afresh at how Descartes expressed himself, find that his ideas do not need to be forced into a modern straitjacket, but may still have something striking and philosophically interesting to say, even when they are allowed to retain their original shape.

5

THE WILL AND FREEDOM

The will simply consists in our ability to do or not do something (that is, to affirm or deny, to pursue or avoid); or rather, it consists simply in the fact that when the intellect puts something forward, we are moved to affirm or deny or to pursue or avoid it in such a way that we do not feel ourselves to be determined by any external force. For in order to be free, there is no need for me to be capable of going in each of two directions; on the contrary, the more I incline in one direction – either because I clearly understand that reasons of truth and goodness point that way, or because of a divinely produced disposition of my inmost thought – the freer is my choice. Neither divine grace nor natural knowledge ever diminishes freedom; on the contrary, they increase and strengthen it. But the indifference I feel when there is no reason pushing me in one direction rather than another is the lowest grade of freedom; it is evidence not of any perfection of freedom, but rather a defect in knowledge, or a kind of negation. For if I always saw clearly what was true and good, I should never have to deliberate about the right judgement or choice; in that case, although I should be wholly free, it would be impossible for me ever to be in a state of indifference.

From these considerations I perceive that the power of willing which I received from God is not, when considered in itself, the cause of my mistakes; for it is both extremely ample and also perfect of its kind. Nor is my power of understanding to blame; for since my understanding comes from God, everything that I understand I undoubtedly understand correctly, and any error here is impossible. So what then is the source of my mistakes? It must simply be this: the scope of the will is wider than that of the intellect; but instead of restricting it within the same limits, I extend its use to matters which I do not understand. Since the will is indifferent in such cases, it easily turns aside from what is true and good, and this is the source of my error and sin . . .

The cause of error must surely be the one I have explained; for if, whenever I have to make a judgement, I restrain my will so that it extends to what the intellect clearly and distinctly reveals, and no further, then it is quite impossible for me to go wrong. This is because every clear and distinct perception is undoubtedly something real and positive, and hence cannot come from nothing, but must necessarily have God for its author. Its author, I say, is God, who is supremely perfect, and who cannot be a deceiver on pain of contradiction; hence the perception is undoubtedly true. So today I have learned not only what precautions to take to avoid ever going wrong, but also what to do to arrive at the truth. For I shall unquestionably reach the truth if only I give sufficient attention to all the things which I perfectly understand, and separate those from all the other cases where my apprehension is more confused and obscure. And this is just what I shall take good care to do from now on.

Meditations on First Philosophy [Meditationes de prima philosophia, 1641]

Extracts from Fourth Meditation (AT 57–8 & 62: CSM II 40 & 43)

One of the common current distortions of Descartes arises from treating him as an 'epistemologist', concerned primarily with the analysis and definition of knowledge. In fact, Descartes conceived of his philosophy as a comprehensive system, not merely focusing on theoretical and cognitive matters, but having practical implications for the human condition and how we should live. Crucial to this latter aspect is his conception of freedom. A prevailing modern conception of free choice sees it as an independent and unconstrained selection between alternative options. Descartes (as the extract above makes clear) conceives of freedom very differently: we are at our freest when we are spontaneously and irresistibly drawn towards a clearly perceived good. This relatively ignored aspect of Descartes's thinking offers a fascinating challenge to the prevailing modern ideal of 'autonomy', as a wholly independent and self-standing power of choice.

Although the implications of all this go far beyond Descartes's theory of knowledge, we do need to set the stage by going back to his quest for certainty. The Cogito gives him his starting point – indubitable awareness of himself as a thinking subject. From a recognition of himself and his own imperfection, he proceeds immediately to an awareness of the divine source of his being. And this opens the door to an entire system of reliable understanding: 'from the contemplation of the true God, in whom all the treasures of wisdom and the sciences lie hidden', he thinks he can see a way forward to the knowledge of other things.

The phrase just quoted, from the opening paragraph of the Fourth Meditation, is, in the Latin wording of Descartes's original text, an almost exact citation from the Bible. In his letter to the Colossians (2:3), St Paul had talked of 'the mystery of God which is Christ, *in whom are hid all the treasures of wisdom and knowledge*' (*in quo sunt omnes thesauri sapientiae et scientiae absconditi*). Descartes, many of whose contemporary readers would have instantly recognized the reference to the Vulgate (the standard Latin text of the Bible), subtly changes the singular *scientiae* ('knowledge') to the plural *scientiarum* ('sciences'). For St Paul, God (in Christ) is the mysterious source of all wisdom; for Descartes, reaching knowledge of God opens the path to 'the sciences'– to true scientific understanding.

The underlying argument is that God, being perfect, and hence incapable of malice or deliberate deception, bestowed a reliable mind on me; so I have reason to trust my mental faculties as essentially accurate. At the very least, I can rely on my most basic and straightforward mathematical intuitions. And since mathematics is the key to physics, the door to science is now open. As Descartes puts it at the close of the Fifth Meditation, 'I can achieve full and certain knowledge of countless matters, including the whole of that physical nature that is the subject-matter of pure mathematics.'

Too good to be true? Doesn't it contradict one of the basic premises that Descartes himself started with – the recognition of his own imperfection? We humans clearly do *not* possess perfect faculties of knowledge and awareness. Indeed, it is surely a plain fact that we do go wrong, if not all the time, at least in a substantial number of our scientific judgements, not to mention our ordinary 'common-sense' beliefs. And mathematical reasoning, as every schoolchild knows, or every adult who struggles to reconcile bank statement with cheque-book stubs, is certainly not immune from this pervasive human tendency to err.

If we are supposed to be the products of a divine and perfect creator, how come our abilities are so limited and imperfect? The problem of our often defective *intellect* is matched by the no less troubling problem of our *moral* defects: how is it that we humans so often do such horribly damaging things to each other? This, of course, is part of a very ancient problem that every theist of the Christian (or Jewish, or Islamic) variety must face – the problem of evil. *Si Deus est, unde malum?* runs the ancient puzzle: 'If there is a God, whence comes the bad?' Can we really suppose that a universe containing so much suffering, sin and error is the creation of a supremely good and perfect God?

The Church fathers had struggled to find a solution to the puzzle by devising what has come to be termed a *theodicy* – a vindication of the justice and goodness of God in the face of the problem of evil. St Augustine (whom, as so often, we find strongly influencing Descartes here) had famously articulated the so-called free will defence: the existence of so much evil was due not to God, but to the evil choices freely made by human beings. And in the Fourth Meditation we find Descartes developing his own theodicy along similar lines. Both intellectual and moral error are due not to any inherent faults in the apparatus bestowed on us by the creator, but to the misuse of our faculty of free will.

Descartes's solution turns out to be an ingenious one. The key to it is the observation in the extract above that *the scope of the will is wider than that of the intellect*. Our intellect is finite, limited. Can we complain about that? No, Descartes replies later on in the Fourth Meditation: 'it is in the nature of a created intellect to be finite'. If God is to bring into being anything besides himself, then reality will include something that falls short of the infinite divine perfection. You could say, of course, that it would have been better for God to rest content with his own supreme, self-sufficient perfection, and not bring anything lesser into existence at all. But that sounds insincere. Most of us regard our human existence, for all its finitude, as better than nothing.

On the other hand, we do have one seemingly infinite faculty: the power of will. It seems to have no limits; indeed, Descartes regards it as quasi-divine – the faculty in which above all 'I bear the image and likeness of God' (AT VII 57: CSM II 40). Our will extends way beyond our limited intellect, since we have the power to agree or disagree with propositions despite the fact that our judgement is often not based on sufficient evidence or an adequate intellectual grasp of the truth. And this, Descartes argues, is the source of error.

You could imagine a being created (or evolved) who would withhold judgement in all cases where the truth was not wholly intellectually transparent. This would be a very dry, very cautious sort of creature. Human beings are rasher than that: they use their freedom to back hunches, to take a chance. They won't restrict themselves to the narrow confines of what their intellects clearly perceive, but constantly reach out and commit themselves. Mistakes, sometimes devastating, can result, but this is the price of freedom. The will extends further than the intellect.

The kind of freedom that Descartes points to here might be called a 'two-way' power – a power of yea or nay. 'Yes, I'll accept that!' 'No, I disagree!' How often do we act in this way, despite the fact that the evidence is thin, or imperfectly grasped? In so doing, we exercise what the medieval philosophers had traditionally called 'freedom of indifference' – the ability to jump one way or the other, 'to affirm or deny, to pursue or avoid', as Descartes puts it. But when, as so often, such decisions are made in the absence of proper supporting reasons, are we really using our will properly? In our passage, Descartes makes a crucial point: 'the indifference I feel when there is no reason pushing me in one direction rather than another is the *lowest grade of freedom*; it is evidence not of any perfection of freedom, but rather a defect in knowledge, or a kind of negation'. Consider the proposition that there is life on other worlds. I can insist that this is true or I can refuse to accept it. But either way, my 'freedom' to decide is really just a sign of ignorance: rationally speaking, there just isn't enough evidence to settle the matter.

Consider now the opposite case, where I perceive the full structure of supporting reasons for some proposition with blinding, transparent clarity (when, for example, I contemplate a proposition like '2 + 2 = 4'). It doesn't look, any more, as if I now have 'freedom of indifference'. No longer do I seem to have the power of 'yea or nay'. Instead of two options, there is now really only one: I must judge: 'Yes, it's true!' In a certain sense, perhaps, we are less independent or 'autonomous' in such situations, but on the other hand, we are freely exercising our rational faculties, and are in what seems to be an ideal situation with respect to both intellect and will: so closely and irresistibly are we in touch with the reasons that support our judgement that we feel a kind of spontaneous flow of rational assent welling up within us. 'Yes, it's true!' This is not freedom of 'indifference', but a quite different kind of freedom – what had traditionally been included under the label 'freedom of spontaneity'. And

Descartes describes it, in our extract, in very honorific terms: 'in order to be free, there is no need for me to be capable of going in each of two directions; on the contrary, the more I incline in one direction – either because I clearly understand that reasons of truth and goodness point that way, or because of a divinely produced disposition of my inmost thought – the freer is my choice'. This is, if you like, the highest grade of human freedom: contemplating the truth so clearly that it is utterly compelling, and our rational understanding leaves us no alternative but to assent.

The success or otherwise of Descartes's implied acquittal of the Creator of responsibility for human error is a complex question. In Descartes's picture we simply have to accept our finitude – the fact that there are many things we grasp only inadequately, if at all. The power of our will gives us the opportunity to be cautious in such cases and withhold judgement, or to take a risk and give our assent or denial. What exactly is there to complain of here if we are writing up an imaginary charge-sheet against our maker? On the other hand, there is also an objective order of truths – for example, mathematical truths – which we have the rational power to grasp; and here, so long as we contemplate the truth, our transparent perceptions bring automatic, spontaneous assent – freedom of spontaneity. Again, Descartes implicitly challenges us to say what exactly we would complain of here. In assenting irresistibly to the transparently clear perceptions of reason, are we not in exactly the situation free and rational beings would most want to be?

All the above reasoning applies equally well to our moral choices in the conduct of life, and not just to abstract intellectual truths. Notice that Descartes, in our extract, couples together *assent* and *denial* (intellectual judgements) and *pursuit* and *avoidance* (moral choices). And his argument applies to 'reasons of goodness' just as much as to 'reasons of truth'. Just as with mathematical truth, so it is with moral truth: there is good, in Descartes's view, that is so transparently valuable and worthy of choice that as soon as we perceive it properly we will spontaneously declare, 'Yes, this is what I should pursue!' And the more fluidly and spontaneously we incline towards such transparently perceived good, 'the freer is our choice'.

So what becomes of the problem of evil? With his model of a kind of blinding light of transparent reason, has Descartes really accounted for the fact that we so often go astray? The answer here is that, for Descartes, so long as we are focused on the relevant truths, or the relevant good, only spontaneous assent is possible. We are, if you like, assimilated to the condition of angelic or heavenly creatures, bathed in light and rejoicing in the transparent presence of truth and goodness. Yet, of course, human beings do not remain constantly focused on the good and the true. Our powers of attention are limited. Moreover, as creatures of flesh and blood, we are distracted by a host of 'interference signals' from the body, which often generate strong inclinations towards objects, like chocolate cream cake or salted French fries (not to mention more serious vices) that seem alluring or desirable, only to turn out later to be bad for us. In short, we are not angelic intellects, but embodied human beings, with all the additional limitations that implies. And it is partly for this reason that humans often get diverted towards lesser good, or only superficially attractive diversions, or even things which are positively bad. Thus, despite the divine 'light of reason' so extolled by Descartes, he would also have agreed with the author of the Fourth Gospel, that human beings are often able to 'prefer the darkness to the light' (John 3:19). To be equipped to examine this recurring theme of the conflict between intellect and passions, we shall first need to look at one of the most problematic parts of Descartes's philosophy – his account of the relation between mind and body.

6

MIND VERSUS BODY

I know that everything which I clearly and distinctly understand is capable of being created by God so as to correspond exactly with my understanding of it. Hence the fact that I can clearly and distinctly understand one thing apart from another is enough to make me certain that the two things are distinct, since they are capable of being separated at least by God . . . Thus, simply by knowing that I exist, and seeing at the same time that absolutely nothing else belongs to my nature of essence except that I am a thinking thing, I can infer correctly that my essence consists solely in the fact that I am a thinking thing. It is true that I may have (or to anticipate, that I certainly have) a body that is very closely joined to me. But nevertheless, on the one hand I have a clear and distinct idea of myself, in so far as I am simply a thinking, non-extended thing; and on the other hand I have a distinct idea of body, in so far as this is simply an extended, non-thinking thing. And accordingly, it is certain that I am really distinct from my body, and can exist without it . . .

There is a great difference between mind and body, inasmuch as the body is by its very nature always divisible, while the mind is utterly indivisible. For when I consider the mind, or myself in so far as I am merely a thinking thing, I am unable to distinguish any parts within myself; I understand myself to be something quite single and complete . . . By contrast, there is no corporeal or extended thing that I can think of which in my thought I cannot

easily divide into parts; and this very fact makes me understand
that it is divisible . . .

Nature teaches me, by these sensations of pain, hunger, thirst
and so on, that I am not merely present in my body as a sailor is
present in a ship, but that I am very closely joined and, as it were,
intermingled with it, so that I and the body form a unit. If this
were not so, I, who am nothing but a thinking thing, would not
feel pain when the body was hurt, but would perceive the damage
purely by the intellect, just as a sailor perceives by sight if anything in his ship is broken.

Meditations on First Philosophy [Meditationes de prima philosophia,
1641]

Extracts from Sixth Meditation (AT VII 78, 86, & 81: CSM II 54, 59 &
56)

Perhaps Descartes's most famous (or notorious) doctrine is what
has come to be known as 'Cartesian dualism' – the view that the
mind is an entirely immaterial substance that (in the words of
the *Discourse on the Method*) 'does not depend on any place, or
depend on any material thing, in order to exist'. The extract
for this chapter presents one of Descartes's main arguments
for this immaterialist view of the mind. What should be our
modern response to it? In particular, what implications does it
have for science, and for religion? Descartes himself believed
that his views could be used to bolster religious faith, but the
theological issues here are not as straightforward as might appear.
As for science, Descartes's dualism has served as a target for
modern physicalist and computational theories of the mind. Is
it really the case, as is often supposed, that these recent develop-
ments make Descartes's views obsolete, since it is supposedly now
possible to explain everything about the mind without invoking
any 'souls', 'spirits' or other immaterial entities?

Let's start with this last question. Modern accounts of the
mind tend generally to presuppose a *naturalist* paradigm: they
make the assumption of a cosmos that is entirely composed of

physical entities (electrons, quarks, stars, planets, molecules, biological organisms and so on), and lay it down as a fundamental principle that all the phenomena we encounter arise merely out of the way these materials behave, and can be wholly explained without recourse to anything supernatural, or 'spooky', to use the fashionably pejorative term often used of entities like 'souls'. Yet what could be more 'spooky' than the mind as conceived of by Descartes – an entirely spiritual substance occupying no space, or (as he puts it in our extract) a 'thinking, non-extended thing'?

To posit immaterial souls or spirits is certainly out of tune with today's scientific worldview. But are they at least a *logical* possibility? Even if we grant that every conscious event in our universe does in actual fact depend on some physical structure (like a brain), is it at least *conceivable* that consciousness could inhere in some non-physical substance? Some modern philosophers and scientists would reject this out of hand; for them, mental states simply *are* physical states of the brain or nervous system (e.g. electrical or chemical states). But others, known as 'functionalists', consider mental properties to be more abstract, organizational properties.

The American philosopher Hilary Putnam was famous in the late twentieth century for his championing of this kind of functionalist account of the mind. Functional states, in this view, are *organizational* or *computational* states, identified by their causal links to one another and to sensory inputs and behavioural outputs. Keeping things at this formal, organizational level, and abstracting from the physical details, enables Putnam to define states like pain in a way that allows that they may be realized in many different kinds of biological structure, provided those structures play the appropriate causal role in the organism's circuitry. For example, when an organism's sensory inputs signal damage to the body, these inputs have a high negative value in the organism's 'preference function'; in other words, the individual in question (which may be a human or an animal or perhaps even made of silicon) is organized in such a way that it attaches great importance to avoiding the noxious stimulus.

The basic idea here is that a good theory of the mind ought to be fairly *neutral* about the precise physical way in which the required organizational states are realized. An alien from another galaxy might have a very different kind of body from us carbon-based life forms, but if it was appropriately organized, if it processed the information in the right way, it ought still to count as thinking – or as enjoying itself, or as being in pain, or whatever. Indeed, so neutral are functionalists about how a system might be realized that their approach does not rule out the possibility that a mental state might be realized by 'a system consisting of a body and a "soul", if such things there be'. (The quotation is from Putnam's paper 'The Nature of Mental States' – (see Suggestions for Further Reading on p. 98 for details.) Functionalism (though clearly inspired by modern computer science) is thus not technically incompatible with Cartesian dualism. According to the functionalist, if it turned out that there were such things as souls, they would certainly qualify as genuinely conscious entities, provided they processed information in the right way.

The point of this excursus into modern philosophy of the mind is that many contemporary theorists, though they would no doubt insist that everything in our world is, in actual fact, physical, nevertheless define the mind in such a way that does not categorically exclude the possibility of a non-physical mental substance. Non-physical minds are at least conceivable. Yet what Descartes is claiming in our passage above is just this: *the logical possibility of a non-physical mind*. His argument is that at least an omnipotent God (who by definition can do anything that is logically possible, or 'clearly and distinctly conceivable') could create a mind utterly distinct from a body. Mind distinct from body is thus, as we would say nowadays, at least theoretically possible. And that fact alone, argues Descartes, is enough to show that mind and body are indeed really distinct.

Descartes's position, then, cannot be dismissed as irredeemably out of date, in the way some modern commentators suppose. Nevertheless, he still owes us arguments to support his claim that mind is genuinely conceivable, clearly and distinctly conceivable, apart from body. Unfortunately for him, one such argument that he produces does not work. The mere fact that I reckon I can somehow imagine a disembodied mind, or imagine myself 'waking up' without a body (see Chapter 3), does not seem enough, on its own, to show that the thinking thing that is 'I' could really exist without the body.

One further argument for the genuine distinctness of mind and body is offered in our present extract from the Sixth Meditation: the mind seems to be utterly *indivisible*, whereas the body is always divisible. This connects with Descartes's conception of the physical world as by definition 'extended' and quantifiable (see Chapter 1). Any piece of matter, anything occupying space, however small it may be, can be divided up into parts. Yet the mind does not seem to be divisible into parts in this way.

The 'divisibility argument' does not seem conclusive. In the first place, some would argue that what Descartes calls 'the mind, or myself' *is* divisible. Sigmund Freud and his many followers in the psychoanalytic tradition typically maintain that parts of my consciousness can be split off, so that they become temporarily or permanently inaccessible. In the second place, we need to be careful to ask what is the subject or substance that is the bearer of consciousness – what is it that is supposed to be *doing the thinking*? Descartes takes himself to have established that the bearer of consciousness is an immaterial mental substance, something that occupies no space, and is therefore not divisible. But if the bearer of consciousness is the whole human being (as Aristotle, for example, would have maintained, together with many modern philosophers of mind), then the mind is not really a substance at all. Rather, though it is grammatically a noun, 'mind' in fact refers to a *property* or *attribute* – something which, like digestion or any other function, does not and cannot exist 'in its own right', as it were. The word 'mind' may look like a noun, but it should really be understood as if it were an adjective: mental functioning is something that can only occur as an attribute or activity of the whole person – the flesh and blood human being who is Joe Bloggs, or René Descartes, or whoever. So Descartes's inability to distinguish any parts within his conscious self still would not necessarily show that the 'self' in question is actually an independent substance in its own right.

We are now getting into fairly abstruse metaphysical territory; but perhaps the above brief discussion is enough to show that Descartes's claim that he is an indivisible mental substance, entirely distinct from the body, is, at the very least, a complex and difficult one, that has all sorts of ramifications. His arguments are certainly controversial and problematic, and they may have many aspects that deserve to be probed and questioned. But whichever way you read them, they cannot just be dismissed out of hand.

What about the theological implications of his mind–body dualism? Many people may initially be inclined to suppose that you need to believe in an immaterial soul in order to make sense of the Christian doctrine of the afterlife; and indeed Descartes himself, in the letter in which he dedicated his *Meditations* to the theology faculty at the Sorbonne, presented himself as a defender of the Christian faith along these lines. Yet the religious implications of asserting the immaterial nature of the mind or soul are in fact not so straightforward. The Apostles' Creed speaks of the afterlife, or the 'life everlasting', but refers to the 'resurrection of the *body*'; it does *not* include any clauses about the survival of a [Cartesian-style] immaterial spirit. What is more, if you start to think about what makes you *you*, and subtract all the attributes that depend on your bodily nature, what you are left with in the end may seem altogether too thin and insubstantial to qualify as the bearer of a genuine future existence in the next world. Could your 'existence' have any real individual character once abstracted from your particular location or perspective, deprived of your specific bodily feelings and visual and auditory and tactile sensations, removed from your *situatedness* in the ordinary bodily circumstances of your life? Those who have hopes of immortality may be ill-advised to rely merely on the continued existence of a Cartesian-style immaterial substance.

Although Descartes is often accused of reducing us simply to immaterial spirits or 'ghosts', he did in fact acknowledge that our concept of a human being necessarily involves an intimate link with the body. His official mind–body dualism does, to be sure, assert that I, considered simply as a 'thinking unextended thing', can be considered in abstraction from any concept of the body; but when I am considered *as a human being*, things are rather different. In the final paragraph of the extract above, the body is described not as a mere optional extra as it were, not as a mere machine or apparatus which the ghostly mind happens to inhabit, but as something with which I am intimately intermingled, so that 'I and the body form a unit'.

I am not just 'present in my body as a sailor is present in a ship'. This is a strange metaphor (whose origins go back to Aristotle); what exactly does Descartes mean by saying our relationship with the body is not of this kind? Imagine that you just *noticed* damage to the body, in a purely intellectual or 'informational' way, as it were, in the way in which a pilot might observe that there was a problem with an engine by scrutinizing a computer printout of fuel consumption or heat output. It's not perhaps beyond our powers to imagine a science-fiction scenario in which alien beings monitored the states of their bodies in this kind of way. But we humans, of course, are not like that. We *might* detect bodily damage purely intellectually, in this fashion – perhaps as a diabetic monitors the level of his or her insulin or blood sugar, by using a special detector, or taking a blood sample for analysis. But in most cases, we detect damage in a much simpler and more vivid and more direct way. If someone starts sawing off your foot, you don't merely detect the damage, or perceive it cognitively, you have an immediate and unmistakable sensation – of *pain*. Sensations are, for Descartes, one of the special signatures of our human status, our status as *essentially embodied beings*.

7

THE HUMAN BEING

When you said that a human being is an 'accidental unity', I know that you meant only what everyone else admits, that a human being is made up of two things which are really distinct. But the expression 'accidental unity' is not used in that sense by the Scholastics. Therefore . . . whenever the occasion arises, in public and in private, you should give out that you believe that a human being is a true entity in its own right, and not an accidental unity, and that the mind is united in a real and substantial manner to the body. You must say that they are united . . . by a true mode of union, as everyone agrees, though nobody explains what this amounts to and so you need not do so either. You could do so, however, as I did in my *Meditations*, by saying that we perceive that sensations such as pain are not pure thoughts of a mind distinct from a body, but confused perceptions of a mind really united to a body. For if an angel were in a human body, it would not have sensations as we do, but would simply perceive the motions which are caused by external objects, and in this way would differ from a real human being.

Letter to Regius, January 1642 (AT III 491: CSMK 206)

I may truly say that the question which your Highness poses [of how the soul, being only a thinking substance, can act upon the nerves and muscles so as to perform bodily actions] seems to me the one which can most properly be put to me in view of my published writings. There are two facts about the human soul on which depend all the knowledge we can have of its nature. The first is that it thinks, the second is that, being united to the body, it can act and be acted upon along with it. About the second I have said hardly anything; I have tried only to make the first well understood. For my principal aim was to prove the distinction between the soul and the body, and to this end only the first was useful, and the second might have been harmful. But because your Highness's vision is so clear that nothing can be concealed from her, I will try now to explain how I conceive the union of the soul and the body and how the soul has the power to move the body . . .

[A]s regards body in particular, we have only the notion of extension which entails the notions of shape and motion; and as regards the soul on its own we have only the notion of thought, which includes the perceptions of the intellect and the inclinations of the will. Lastly, as regards the soul and the body together, we have only the notion of their union, on which depends our notion of the soul's power to move the body, and the body's power to act on the soul and cause its sensations and passions . . .

There are thus three kinds of primitive ideas or notions, each of which is known in its own proper manner . . . The soul is conceived only by the pure intellect; body (i.e. extension, shapes and motions) can likewise be known by the intellect alone, but better by the intellect aided by the imagination; and finally, what belongs to the union of the soul and the body is known only obscurely by the intellect alone, or even by the intellect aided by the imagination, but it is known very clearly by the senses . . . Metaphysical thoughts, which exercise the pure intellect, help to familiarize us with the notion of the soul; and the study of mathematics, which exercises the imagination in the consideration of shapes and motions, accustoms us to form a very distinct notion of body. But it is the ordinary course of life

and conversation, and abstention from meditation ... that
teaches us how to conceive of the union of the soul and the
body.

Letters to Elizabeth, 21 May and 28 June 1643 (AT III 664–5 & 691:
CSMK 217–18 & 226–7)

Descartes's dualism was stigmatized by the twentieth-century
British philosopher Gilbert Ryle as the doctrine of 'the ghost in
the machine'; in this interpretation, Descartes regards human
beings as incorporeal souls mysteriously lodged in mechanical
bodies. Descartes himself, however, maintained that the human
being, compounded of mind and body, was a genuine 'substantial union'. What exactly did he mean by this notion? The
extracts in this chapter, from letters to two of his many philosophical correspondents, throw a fascinating light on 'Cartesian
anthropology' – the way Descartes conceived of our human
nature. It turns out that according to him our sensations and
emotions form a distinct category, comprising *irreducibly psy-*
chophysical attributes, which cannot be assimilated either to pure
mental events on the one hand, or to pure physiological
responses on the other. Descartes's theory of the human being
thus turns out to be considerably more complex and subtle than
modern caricatures of his views suggest.

Let us begin with Descartes's remarks to Regius. Henricus
Regius (or Henri Le Roy) was an enthusiastic supporter of
Descartes's ideas on physics and physiology, and was appointed to
the Chair of Medicine at the University of Utrecht in 1638. His
championing of Cartesian ideas led to bitter disputes with his
colleague in the Chair of Theology, Gisbertus Voetius, an
implacable foe of the Cartesian system; and the somewhat anx-
ious tone of Descartes's remarks in our extract reflects his fear
that Regius's often brash and oversimplified advocacy of his ideas
would implicate him in unending theological controversies.

The orthodox scholastic position, based on the principles laid
down by Aquinas, had insisted on the *unity* of the human being:

in the philosophical jargon, a human was an *ens per se*, a genuine substance or entity in its own right. The mind or soul, by contrast, was (Aquinas had argued) merely an 'incomplete substance' – something that was a part of the whole human being, and, even after death, remained essentially lacking something, since it remained by its nature 'apt' for being united with a body. Descartes's dualistic ideas seemed to go against this, by conceiving of the conscious mind or soul (in this kind of context he uses the two terms interchangeably) as a wholly independent entity, something which, so to speak, merely *happened* to have a body, but could do just as well without it. Regius, in his characteristically over-enthusiastic manner, had trumpeted this Cartesian view as the doctrine that a human being was merely an 'accidental unity' – in the jargon, an *ens per accidens.*

The terminology may seem abstruse to us now, but Regius's interpretation of Descartes is not very different from that of Gilbert Ryle. Asserting that a human is an 'accidental unity' comes down to saying that in Descartes's view I am really no more than a ghost in a machine, an immaterial spirit that happens to inhabit a bodily structure. Descartes's brilliant contemporary Antoine Arnauld had spotted the problem earlier still, in the elegant Fourth Set of Objections that were published along with Descartes's *Meditations* in 1641. It seems, wrote Arnauld in the Fourth Objections,

> that [Descartes's] argument . . . takes us back to the Platonic view . . . that nothing corporeal belongs to our essence, so that man is merely a rational soul and the body merely a vehicle for the soul – a view which gives rise to the definition of man as a *soul that makes use of a body* (*anima corpore utens*). (AT VII 203: CSM II 143)

Plato, to whom Arnauld refers here, was certainly an uncompromising soul–body dualist; and it is interesting that Descartes's unacknowledged intellectual mentor St Augustine, himself strongly influenced by Plato, defines a human being as a 'rational soul *using* a mortal and earthly body' (*De moribus ecclesiae catholicae* [AD 387/9], 1.27.52).

In responding to Arnauld, Descartes firmly rebuts the Platonic interpretation of his views, just as (one imagines) he would have repudiated Ryle's 'ghost in the machine' label were he alive today. Despite the special and distinct nature of the mind or soul, Descartes wants to insist that a human being is indeed a genuine unified entity, an *ens per se*, not merely an *ens per accidens*: mind and body are united 'in a real and substantial manner' by a 'true mode of union'. If an angel (i.e. an incorporeal spirit) were in a human body, 'it would not have sensations as we do, but would simply perceive the motions which are caused by external objects, and in this way would differ from a real human being'. The real human being, what he elsewhere called *le vrai homme*, is for Descartes genuinely *incarnate* – that is to say, essentially and really an embodied creature of flesh and blood – and our distinctive human repertoire of feeling and sensation and emotion is the surest sign of that.

But can Descartes have it both ways? If he thinks he has arguments to establish the utter *distinctness* of mind and body, how can he also assert their *union*? In a letter to Princess Elizabeth, from which our second extract is taken, he attempts to resolve the problem. Elizabeth, former Princess of Bohemia, but exiled to the Netherlands (where Descartes himself resided for most of his adult life), was one of Descartes's acutest critics, and their famous correspondence includes several letters on this very matter of the relationship of mind and body.

In explaining himself to Elizabeth, Descartes describes not two but *three* primitive notions: soul, body and, third, their union. The first two are known by the intellect, but the third is known by ordinary experience. So, although intellectual philosophizing establishes the distinction between mind and body, it is everyday sensation that shows us the union. This links up with the point made to Regius: we know by our sensations that we are not pure intellects, not angels inhabiting bodies; for the *way* in which we are made aware of our bodily states (through pain or hunger, for example) has a direct and immediate character, a 'phenomenology', as modern philosophers put it, that defies rational analysis, but is certainly not just a matter of pure intellectual awareness.

One might object at this point that Descartes is mired in a contradiction. If the evidence from the ordinary external and internal senses testifies to some immediate intermingling or union of mind and body, then surely there must be something wrong with the intellectual arguments that are supposed to establish the utter distinctness of mind and body. Again, Descartes surely cannot have it both ways. Or, to put the point another way, in acknowledging our human status as genuine unities, is he not admitting something of a mystery, something which his official dualistic arguments cannot really explain?

In the founding narrative of the religious culture in which Descartes was brought up, one very special manifestation of the relationship between spirit and matter was, of course, already shrouded in mystery. God, the supreme, eternal and immaterial spirit, had taken bodily flesh in Jesus Christ. The Incarnation was not claimed to be something wholly transparent to reason; on the contrary, it was universally acknowledged as a *magnum mysterium*, a 'great and mighty marvel'. Descartes himself had reflected on this in a notebook that has survived from his formative travels in Europe as a young man of twenty-three: 'The Lord has made three marvels: things out of nothing, free will, and God in Man' (AT X 218: CSM I 5). Here, the Incarnation, God's taking bodily form, is interestingly compared with the mystery of Creation itself, whereby something material was brought into being by God *ex nihilo*, out of nothing. So the relationship of God to his material creation, and his subsequently entering that creation in bodily form, were central mysteries of the Christian faith on which the young Descartes had pondered at a crucial stage of his early adulthood. Much later, in the Sixth

Meditation, Descartes was to explore a far more familiar and mundane version of the spirit–matter relation – its manifestation in our ordinary experience of human situatedness in a material environment, and – even closer to hand – the relation each of us has to 'the body which by some special right I call "mine"' (AT VII 76: CSM II 52).

There is, then, something in the human condition that remains mysterious for Descartes, or at least not wholly transparent to philosophical analysis. Nevertheless, his account to Elizabeth of 'three primitive notions' has a certain appeal, provided we can reconcile this 'trialism', as it may be called, with the dualism of mind and body that his official arguments insist upon.

One way of understanding Descartes's insistence on this *third* primitive notion (the notion of a mind–body union in addition to the notions of body and of mind) is in *attributive* terms. Substantially speaking, there are only two kinds of things – mind and body; this is the standard dualistic claim. But Descartes is also telling us, in effect, that the human being, the mind–body complex, is, in its own right, the bearer of distinctive and irreducible *attributes,* or *properties*. In this sense we might say that water is a 'primitive' notion, meaning that it is not a mere mixture but a genuine compound, possessing attributes 'in its own right' (distinctive 'watery' characteristics that cannot be reduced to the properties of the hydrogen or oxygen which make it up). Or, as Descartes puts it in *Principles*, while he recognizes only 'two ultimate classes of things', thinking things and extended things, nevertheless the appetites, passions, and sensations, which arise from the close and intimate union of the two, are items which 'must not be referred either to the mind alone or the body alone' (*Principia philosophiae* [1644], Part I, article 48).

Just as the 'watery' properties of water (for example, its liquidity at ten degrees Celsius, or its pleasantness to drink) will not figure in the list of properties either of hydrogen or of oxygen on their own, so our embodied sensations (hunger, thirst, pleasure, pain, etc.) will not figure in a complete list either of thoughts on the one hand (understanding, willing, and so on), or of modes of extension (size, shape, etc.) on the other. Our feelings and passions, signatures of our necessarily embodied status as human beings, are properties that arise when a mind is united to a body, just as the watery properties of water arise when hydrogen is compounded with oxygen. In each case there are two and only two substances (mind and body, or hydrogen and oxygen); but for all that, we can say with perfect coherence, and indeed truth, that when the two are compounded into a 'genuine union', then distinct and irreducible properties of a third kind come into being.

Descartes's understanding of the special nature of human beings has crucial implications for morality. Previous ethical systems developed by the Greeks tended to take on a 'ratiocentric' bias, which led to problems about applying a rationally devised life-plan to the awkward realm of human feeling and emotion. The Cartesian model for science seems at first to be even more ratiocentric, viewing the world as an abstract, mathematically ordered system of 'extended matter in motion', and construing the human contemplators of that system as pure thinking things, detached from the world of extension, and alienated even from the physical mechanisms of their own bodies. But Descartes's distinctive 'anthropology', his account of the human being as a genuine unity, puts all this in a rather different focus. Although intellectual analysis reveals a stark dualism of extended matter on the one hand and incorporeal consciousness on the other, our own daily experience as human beings provides a very different perspective – that of the 'substantial union' of mind and body. Far from operating as the pilot of an alien bodily machine, each one of us finds the operations of the body that is in an intimate sense his or her own generating a vivid human tapestry of sensations and emotions. And the ordering and management, and proper enjoyment, of these feelings will be an essential ingredient of the good life for human beings.

Ethics, then, will have its own distinct subject matter – a subject matter which is irreducible in the sense that it cannot be fully understood in terms either of the mathematical descriptions of physics, or of the purely intellectual and volitional operations of the mind. To understand what makes us most fully and distinctively human, we have to lay aside the intellectually analysed categories of thought and extension, and focus on the emotional dimension that characterizes our daily experience as creatures of flesh and blood.

8

THE ANIMAL WORLD

I cannot share the opinion of Montaigne and others who attribute understanding or thought to animals. I am not worried that people say that human beings have absolute dominion over all the other animals; for I agree that some of them are stronger than us, and I believe that there may also be some animals which have a natural cunning capable of deceiving the shrewdest human beings. But I consider that they imitate or surpass us only in those of our actions which are not guided by our thought. It often happens that we walk or eat without thinking at all about what we are doing; and similarly, without using our reason, we reject things which are harmful for us, and parry the blows aimed at us. Indeed, even if we expressly willed not to put our hands in front of our head when we fall, we could not prevent ourselves. I consider also that if we had no thought then we would walk, as the animals do, without having learned to; and it is said that those who walk in their sleep sometimes swim across streams in which they would drown if they were awake. As for the movements of our passions, even though in us they are accompanied by thought because we have the faculty of thinking, it is nevertheless very clear that they do not depend on thought, because they often occur in spite of us. Consequently they can also occur in animals, even more violently than they do in human beings, without our being able to conclude from that that animals have thoughts.

In fact, none of our external actions can show anyone who examines them that our body is not just a self-moving machine but contains a soul with thoughts, with the exception of spoken words, or other signs that have reference to particular topics without expressing any passion. I say 'spoken words or other signs', because deaf-mutes use signs as we use spoken words; and I say that these signs must have reference, to exclude the speech of parrots, without excluding the speech of madmen, which has reference to particular topics even though it does not follow reason. I add also that these words or signs must not express any passion, to rule out not only cries of joy or sadness and the like, but also whatever can be taught by training to animals. If you teach a magpie to say good-day to its mistress when it sees her approach, this can only be by making the utterance of this word the expression of one of its passions. For instance it will be an expression of the hope of eating, if it has always been given a titbit when it says it. Similarly, all the things which dogs, horses, and monkeys are taught to perform are only expressions of their fear, their hope, or their joy; and consequently they can be performed without any thought. Now it seems to me very striking that the use of words, so defined, is something peculiar to human beings. Montaigne and Charron may have said that there is a greater difference between one human being and another than between a human being and an animal; yet there has never been known an animal so perfect as to use a sign to make other animals understand something which bore no relation to its passions; and there is no human being so imperfect as not to do so, since even deaf-mutes invent special signs to express their thoughts. This seems to me a very strong argument to prove that the reason why animals do not speak as we do is not that they lack the organs but that they have no thoughts. It cannot be said that they speak to each other but we cannot understand them; for since dogs and some other animals express their passions to us, they would express their thoughts also if they had any.

I know that animals do many things better than we do, but this does not surprise me. It can even be used to prove that they act naturally and mechanically, like a clock which tells the time better than our judgement does. Doubtless when the swallows come in spring, they operate like clocks. The actions of honey-bees are of the same nature; so also is the discipline of cranes in flight, and of apes in fighting, if it is true that they keep discipline. Their instinct to bury their dead is no stranger than that of dogs and cats who scratch the earth for the purpose of burying their excrement; they hardly ever actually bury it, which shows that they act only by instinct and without thinking. The most that one can say is that though the animals do not perform any action which shows us that they think, still, since the organs of their bodies are not very different from ours, it may be conjectured that there is attached to these organs some thought such as we experience in ourselves, but of a very much less perfect kind. To this I have nothing to reply except that if they thought as we do, they would have an immortal soul like us. This is unlikely, because there is no reason to believe it of some animals without believing it of all, and many of them such as oysters and sponges are too imperfect for this to be credible.

From the letter to the Marquess of Newcastle, 23 November 1646 (AT IV 573–6: CSMK 302–4)

Descartes, together with many of his disciples, had few if any reservations about the use of animal vivisection to further medical and physiological research. A standard modern interpretation sees such practices as drawing support from Descartes's supposed doctrine of the *bête-machine* – the view that non-human animals are simply mechanical automata, devoid of conscious sensation of any kind. Yet the modern concept of an automaton (roughly, an insentient 'robot') is very different from that current in the seventeenth century. If we look carefully at this chapter's extract we will see that his position is more nuanced than today's critics tend to suppose.

Non-human animals were one of Descartes's enduring scientific interests, dating from the days when he lived in Kalverstraat (the butchers' quarter) in Amsterdam, and regularly ordered veal carcasses to be brought to his house for dissection. Later on, working on the problem of the circulation of the blood, Descartes performed vivisections on dogs and rabbits; and many Cartesian disciples who did likewise may have allayed any ethical scruples they had by reflecting that the squeaks of their victims were of no more significance than the fact that a church organ makes a certain sound when you press one of the keys (cf. AT IX 165: CSM I 104).

Nevertheless, Descartes's considered stance on whether non-human animals have *feelings* or *passions* turns out to be quite complicated. The main question discussed in the letter quoted above is whether animals *think* – whether we should attribute faculties like judgement and deliberation to them. And he is surely right in pointing out that when the swallows come in spring, this should not be attributed to any kind of thinking, but is something more 'natural' and 'mechanical'. (For the contrasting views of his predecessor and compatriot Michel de Montaigne, whom Descartes targets here, compare Montaigne's 'Apology for Raymond Sebond', in his *Essais* [1580], II, 12.)

Later in the passage above, Descartes goes on to consider a possible argument of his opponents: since the bodies of animals are so like ours, might not some elementary kind of thought be 'attached to these organs'? Descartes rejects this argument on the grounds that if similarity of organs is a reason for allowing the possible presence of thought, then it would be a reason for assigning a 'rational soul' to all animals: 'there is no reason to believe it of some animals without believing it of all, and many of them, such as oysters and sponges, are too imperfect for this to be credible'. This seems a bit of a muddle; Descartes's opponents could surely just deny that oysters and sponges are anatomically similar in the relevant respects, and thus resist the implied slippery slope. In fact Descartes is being a little mischievous here, since he was well aware of the difference between creatures which operate merely in an entirely reflex fashion and those with more complex processing abilities. He elsewhere discusses quite advanced animal behaviour, such as a sheep seeing a wolf and running away (AT VII 230: CSM I 161). His point about such complicated behaviour is, again, that it need not presuppose *thought*; it is simply part of a large repertoire of activities which animals (and indeed often human beings too) engage in 'automatically', including, for example, 'the reception by the external sense organs of light, sounds, smells, tastes, heat and other such qualities, the imprinting of ideas of these qualities in the organ of . . . the imagination, the retention or stamping of these ideas in the memory, the internal movements of the appetites and passions, and finally the external movements of all the limbs which aptly follow both the actions and objects presented to the senses and also the passions and impressions found in the memory' (AT XI 202: CSM I 108). Animals process information, as we do; they learn from previous experience; they are alerted by sight and hearing to the presence of predators; they run away; but none of this requires thought or rationality.

So far so good; but if all animal behaviour is automatic in this sense, does not this imply that animals are mere zombies, lacking any passion or feeling? The short answer is no; those many critics who complain that Descartes relegates animals to the status of automata are over-simplifying. An 'automaton', in seventeenth-century usage, is merely a *self-moving* thing – that is, something which can initiate movements in accordance with some internal principle, or organization of its organs, without needing to be shoved around from the outside. All that Descartes's position implies is that the explanation of animal behaviour is to be found entirely in terms of the organization and functioning of the various intricate internal organs, without reference to any external puppeteer, and without any need to posit a 'rational soul' – a thinking process of the kind found in humans. I do not think there are many people who, on reflection, would disagree with any of this.

In evaluating Descartes's approach to animals we need to bear in mind that a scientific *explanation* of a phenomenon in terms of underlying structures does not necessarily *eliminate* the phenomenon to be explained or *reduce* it to the 'mere' operation of the underlying structures. If I explain the anger of my dog or the fear of my cat by reference to movements of vapour through the nerves (as Descartes does), or the rather more sophisticated apparatus of electrical impulses and the secretion of hormones (as modern biologists do), none of this denies the truth of the original statements, 'Fido is angry' or 'Felix is frightened'. In such an explanation, there need be no 'relegation' of Fido or Felix to the status of a zombie, any more than in explaining the properties of a medicine by reference to its molecular structure I am denying its genuine healing function, or somehow 'relegating' it to the status of a pseudo-medicine, a bunch of 'mere' chemicals.

Even when the faculties of thought and reason are not involved, and even when seemingly 'thoughtful' activities are in fact performed entirely by an automatic subroutine, there still has to be a vast amount of information-processing, and this in turn requires a neural centre where messages from the body are handled. Descartes's dissections of animals were often focused on the complicated neural pathways leading from limbs to brain, and from brain back to muscles. The almost miraculously complex things we can do without conscious direction – and the point applies equally to our fellow creatures in the animal kingdom – shows just how intricate a purely 'mechanical' process in nature can be, and how far the resulting phenomena exceed the capacity of those lumbering machines constructed by human craftsmen. To have the status of a machine 'made by the hand of God' (as Descartes described human and animal bodies in the *Discourse*) is to be something worthy of awe and wonder.

But what about *feelings*? We have seen that Descartes thought human feelings arise from the 'union' or 'intermingling' of soul and body. What is it like, then, for animals, who lack any rational soul, even though they may have complicated nervous systems like ours, which enable them to process information and engage in complex behavioural repertoires like seeking food, escaping from danger, and so on? Again, the standard interpretation of Descartes is that he believes no feelings whatever occur in animals: they are mere robots or zombies. But if we look at the passage above, his position, once more, seems less dogmatic. First of all, he explicitly says in the first paragraph that passions occur in animals 'even more violently than they do in human beings'. Developing this further, he discusses the fact that animals can be trained to do things. How? By rewards and punishments: if you teach a magpie to say 'good-day' to its mistress when it sees her approach, this 'can only be by making the utterance of this word the *expression of one of its passions*'. For instance, it will be an expression of the 'hope of eating', if it has always been rewarded for saying the word. Descartes goes on to say that all the things which dogs, horses, and monkeys are taught to perform are '*only expressions of their fear, their hope, or their joy*'.

Animals, then, *do*, it appears, have feelings like hunger, fear, hope, joy, in Descartes's view. Admittedly, these phenomena are ones Descartes thinks can be explained in complex physiological terms; but *explaining* something, as we have seen, does not entail *eliminating* it, or denying it.

But what is it *like* for a non-rational being to be hungry or be frightened? This is the kind of question that modern philosophers interested in consciousness constantly ask. They talk about a 'subjective' or 'qualitative' or 'phenomenological' dimension to consciousness – about what it is *like* to smell coffee, or taste chocolate, or scratch your foot on a thorn. A celebrated paper by the contemporary American philosopher Thomas Nagel asked, 'What is it like to be a bat?' (He chose bats because they have a special perceptual mechanism – namely, echolocation, which enables them to navigate as they fly, but which we cannot really imagine or experience.) And Nagel's conclusion was that consciousness has a specific, subjective character that can never be discovered just by an 'external' scientific examination of the physiology or information-processing mechanisms of the organism.

These kinds of question are ones which Descartes did not raise. He did once speak about hunger as an 'I-know-not-what tugging' in the stomach (Sixth Meditation), and this phrase suggests he did have a sense of the mysterious 'inner' quality of passions or sensations like hunger. But he was more interested, as a scientist, in investigating the neural and structural and behavioural basis for complex animal behaviour than in speculating on its 'inner' dimensions. We may say that is a philosophical weakness in his approach (although by no means all philosophers would agree). But what we should *not* do is to read Descartes's discussion of animals with modern, Nagel-style, subjectivist spectacles, and then complain that he regards animals as zombies, just because as a scientist he focuses on animal neurology and physiology.

Descartes himself kept a dog, called 'Monsieur Grat': the anthropomorphic name suggests, at the very least, that he must have related to it with some kind of affection. It is thus one of the ironies of history that his doctrine of the 'animal machine' is so often used as a basis for attributing to him a cruel and heartless conception of dogs and cats as mere 'robots'. The record of philosophers with respect to our fellow creatures in the animal kingdom is, it has to be said, not particularly inspiring. The best Immanuel Kant can do for animals is to argue that those who mistreat them are bad because they are likely to go on to mistreat humans (*Lectures on Ethics* 1775–80, Part B, section ix). Jeremy Bentham's utilitarian calculus notoriously allows animals no rights whatever; in the chilling phrase of utilitarian champion Peter Singer, they are 'replaceable'. Against this background it is by no means clear that Descartes should be cast as the philosophical villain. What we can unequivocally say is that he was adamant that animals do not *think*. Exactly what this means, and why he held this view, will be the topic of the next chapter.

9

LANGUAGE AND THOUGHT

[In my *Treatise on Man*] I showed what structure the nerves and muscles of the human body must have in order to make the animal spirits inside them strong enough to move its limbs – as when we see severed heads continue to move about and bite the earth although they are no longer alive. ['Animal spirits' were the fine vapour or gas which Descartes supposed to be the medium for transmission of nerve impulses.] I have indicated what changes must occur in the brain in order to cause waking, sleep and dreams; how light, sounds, smells, tastes, heat and the other qualities of external objects can imprint various ideas on the brain through the mediation of the senses; and how hunger, thirst and the other internal passions can also send their ideas there . . . This will not seem at all strange to those who know how many kinds of automatons, or moving machines, the skill of man can construct with the use of very few parts, in comparison with the great multitude of bones, muscles, nerves, arteries, veins and all the other parts that are in the body of an animal. For they will regard this body as a machine which having been made by the hand of God, is incomparably better ordered than any machine that can be devised by man, and contains in itself movements more wonderful than those in any such machine.

I made special efforts to show that if any such machines had the organs and outward shape of a monkey or of some other animal that lacks reason, we should have no means of knowing that they did not possess entirely the same nature as these animals; whereas if any such machine bore a resemblance to our bodies and imitated our actions as closely as possible for all practical purposes, we should still have two very certain means of recognizing that they were not real humans. The first is that they could never use words, or put together other signs, as we do in order to declare our thoughts to others. For we can certainly conceive of a machine so constructed that it utters words, and even utters words which correspond to bodily action causing a change in its organs (e.g. if you touch it in one spot it asks what you want of it, if you touch it in another it cries out that you are hurting it, and so on). But it is not conceivable that such a machine should produce different arrangements of words so as to give an appropriately meaningful answer to whatever is said in its presence, as the dullest of men can do. Secondly, even though such machines might do some things as well as we do them, or perhaps even better, they would inevitably fail in others, which would reveal that they were acting not through understanding but only from the disposition of their organs. For whereas reason is a universal instrument which can be used in all kinds of situations, these organs need some particular disposition for each particular action; hence it is for all practical purposes impossible for a machine to have enough different organs to make it act in all the contingencies of life in the way which our reason makes us act.

Now in just these two ways we can also know the difference between man and beast. For it is quite remarkable that there are no men so dull-witted or stupid – and this includes even madmen – that they are incapable of arranging various words together and forming an utterance from them in order to make their thoughts understood; whereas there is no other animal, however perfect and well endowed it may be, that can do the like. This does not happen because they lack the necessary organs; for we see that magpies and parrots can utter words as we do, and yet they cannot speak as we do: that is, they cannot show that they are thinking what they are saying. On the other hand, men born deaf and dumb, and thus deprived of speech-organs as much as the beasts, or even more so, normally invent their own signs to make themselves understood by those who are regularly in their company and have the time to learn their language. This shows not merely that the beasts have less reason than humans but that they have no reason at all. For it patently requires very little reason to be able to speak; and since as much inequality can be observed among the animals of a given species as among human beings, and some animals are more easily trained than others, it would be incredible that a superior specimen of the monkey or parrot species should not be able to speak as well as the stupidest child – or at least as well as a child with a defective brain – if their souls were not completely different in nature from ours.

And we must not confuse speech with the natural movements which express passions and which can be imitated by machines as well as by animals. Nor should we think, like some of the ancients, that the beasts speak, although we do not understand their language. For if that were true, then since they have many organs that correspond to ours, they could make themselves understood by us as well as by their fellows. It is also a very remarkable fact that although many animals show more skill than we do in some of their actions, yet the same animals show none at all in many others; so what they do better does not prove that they have any intelligence, for if it did then they would have more intelligence than any of us and would excel us in everything. It proves rather that they have no intelligence at all, and that it is nature which acts in them according to the disposition of their organs. In the same way a clock, consisting only of wheels and springs, can count the hours and measure time more accurately than we can with all our wisdom.

After that, I described the rational soul, and showed that, unlike the other things of which I had spoken, it cannot be

derived in any way from the potentiality of matter, but must be
specially created.

From Discourse on the Method *[Discours de la méthode, 1637], Part V*

(AT VI 55–9: CSM I 139–41)

The study of language has been at the centre of much modern
philosophy, and, as with so many aspects of our modern worldview, the views of Descartes are a crucial part of the background.
The extract above shows how, in a remarkable anticipation of
some of the ideas of the contemporary American linguistic
theorist Noam Chomsky, Descartes insists on the special status
of linguistic output, as opposed to other forms of behaviour,
as the key to what separates human beings from other animals.
Descartes's central insight is that genuine linguistic utterance
is not correlated to specific stimuli; and this means, according to
him, that there is a radical difference between human speech and
the various kinds of signals emitted by non-human animals.

The idea of words as 'signs' (as in Descartes's magpie example
in Chapter 8) might seem to encourage the thought that language
is not a specifically human phenomenon; for do not animals
produce noises that are signs of their desires and emotions, showing they are afraid, for example, or hungry? Descartes, however,
draws a radical distinction between animal utterance and genuine
speech. As we saw in the previous chapter, Descartes in his
scientific inquiries was very interested in the physiological basis
of animal and human behaviour, and held that much of it could
be explained in mechanical terms – rather as the workings of
a clock can be explained by examining its cogs and wheels. In a
phrase that must have been shocking to many of his contempo-
raries, he suggests in our present extract that there is nothing
in the repertoire of a dog or cat that could not in principle be
replicated by an artificial machine; indeed, he goes so far as to
propose that the body (whether human or animal) is really no
more than a machine – albeit a very complex one, 'made by the
hand of God'. Yet Descartes insists that although a mechanical

dog might be possible, one could never have a mechanical human being.

It is *language* that is the key indicator of this non-mechanical aspect of our humanity, and in our extract Descartes points to some crucial features of genuine human language that set it apart from animal utterance. Language has a complex synthetic structure: its components are put together in intricate patterns to make up meaningful propositions, and it is 'not conceivable that . . . a machine should produce different arrangements of words so as to give an appropriately meaningful answer to whatever is said in its presence'. Admittedly, a dog might be trained in a circus to produce a certain number of barks on a specific command, or a bird might naturally emit certain sounds in particular circumstances (for example, a warning signal); but Descartes argues in effect that this will always be a patterned response to a given stimulus, whereas genuine language is stimulus-free. Descartes links this creative aspect of language, whereby we are able to talk about each new contingency that arises in life, to our use of the 'universal instrument of reason': in other words, language is intimately related to thought and understanding.

In the light of our knowledge of how much in common we have with the higher animals, it may seem difficult to accept the Cartesian thesis that our linguistic capacity puts a great gulf between them and us. Descartes's arguments, however, are not easy to counter. Given that genuine linguistic output is potentially infinite in its versatility and scope, it follows that it differs radically from the finite outputs of animals, that are always closely correlated to the stimulus of a specific input.

Descartes developed his ideas further in a letter to the Cambridge Platonist Henry More, dated 5 February 1649:

In my opinion the main reason for holding that animals lack thought is the following. Within a single species some of them are more perfect than others, as humans are too. This can be seen in horses and dogs, some of which learn what they are taught much better than others; and all animals easily communicate to us, by voice or bodily movement, their natural impulses of anger, fear, hunger and so on. Yet in spite of all these facts, it has never been observed that any brute animal has attained the perfection of using real speech, that is to say, of indicating by word or sign something relating to thought alone and not to natural impulse. *Such speech is the only sure sign of thought hidden within a body.* All human beings use it, however stupid and insane they may be, even though they may have no tongue and organs of voice; but no animals do. Consequently this can be taken as a real specific difference between humans and animals. (AT V 278: CSMK 366, emphasis added)

Despite the phrase 'hidden within the body', Descartes's language argument, properly construed, is *not* an argument about how linguistic competence provides plausible evidence for the occurrence of an essentially *private* process. It is based on an analysis of what it is to think – namely, that it involves an indefinitely rich, stimulus-free capacity to respond to 'all the contingencies of life': it is based, in other words, on a gap between input and output, as observed *from the outside*. Genuinely linguistic competence, the creation every day of new sentences, unlinked to specific behavioural stimuli, is something which could not in principle be produced by a purely mechanical automaton. There is nothing in these arguments that invokes the picture of thought as a mysterious inner process accessible only to the subject.

Nevertheless, the talk of thought 'hidden within the body' does conjure up the spectre of what modern philosophers disparagingly call 'Cartesian privacy' – the idea of thought as an essentially hidden process, of which speech is merely the outward sign. As noted in Chapter 3, the main tenor of contemporary philosophy has been highly hostile to the conception of language and thought as subjective or private processes, and one may be tempted to read Descartes's term 'hidden' as indicating something in principle unobservable, and something accessible only to the subject. But that is by no means the only possible meaning of the term. The compelling idea of the scientist as an investigator of something 'hidden' (*latens*) had been presented some thirty years earlier by Francis Bacon (whom we know Descartes had read), in his *Novum Organum* (1620). The true 'work and aim of human knowledge', wrote Bacon, is the quest for a 'hidden schematism' (*latens schematismus*); the scientist's job is to look for the micro processes and configurations of matter, which are responsible for the behaviour of all observed physical phenomena (Book II, § 1). 'Latent' here does not imply anything occult or private: the explanatory structures uncovered by empirical science are 'hidden' only in the sense that they are not readily observable at the macro level. What the scientist does, starting from careful observation of the phenomena, is to theorise about the possible fine structures which might be responsible for what is observed, with the eventual goal of bringing what is initially hidden into the light.

This, of course, is precisely the aim of Descartes in all his scientific work. To explain magnetism, fire, the beating of the heart, growth, respiration, even vision, and purposive behaviour like the sheep's running away from the wolf (as discussed in Chapter 8), Descartes offered explanations in terms of the minute interactions of particles too small to be observed with the naked eye. The high-velocity interactions of the tiny particles he called 'subtle matter' are, he reasoned, the unobserved causes responsible for light; the spirallings of screw-shaped molecules are responsible for magnetism; the pneumatic pressures of neural gas are responsible for reflex behaviour in humans and animals; intricate brain events are responsible for more complicated goal-seeking action.

In the case of reasoning and language Descartes saw no way forward for the physical scientist. He does at least consider here in the *Discourse* the possibility of a bodily 'instrument' of reason. But what made a physical realization of such an instrument hard for him to envisage was, at least partly, a matter of *number and size* – of how many structures of the appropriate kind could be packed into a given part of the body. Descartes was a keen anatomist, and his dissections of the brain and nervous system had revealed the operation of tiny structures which he believed had considerable explanatory power. But he was committed to the essential underlying simplicity of those structures. Everything going on in the brain worked by means of elementary 'push and pull operations', not in principle any different from the operations of cogs and levers that could be observed in the ordinary macro world. The elementary laws of mechanics were the same laws that operated throughout in the universe (AT VI 54: CSM I 139). Committed as he was to this homogeneous and simplified model of all physical interaction, Descartes could not envisage the brain or nervous system as being capable of the complexity necessary to produce genuine thought and language.

So Descartes was driven to suppose that the hidden schematism responsible for thought was something mysterious and incorporeal – the 'rational soul'. It is interesting to speculate on whether, had he been alive today, he might have abandoned his belief in an incorporeal soul responsible for thought and language. The language argument in our extract from the *Discourse* hinges on the practical impossibility of a physical mechanism possessing a *sufficiently large number of different parts* (*assez de divers organes*) to facilitate the indefinite range of human responses to 'all the contingencies of life'. Modern neurophysiology, one might suppose, has answered this particular worry by revealing the mind-boggling multiplicity of connections within the cerebral cortex, estimated at over ten billion.

Even in the face of this, Descartes might still have maintained that a purely physical structure could not generate the relevant kind of plasticity and innovativeness necessary for genuine linguistic output. Matters are complicated, however, by the fact that Descartes's view of what matter might or might not do was coloured by a very crude conception of material stuff as pure geometrical extension, so there must be an element of speculation in trying to transfer his arguments to the context of our far richer contemporary physics. However that may be, there is no doubt that Descartes's general scientific quest was for latent (in Bacon's benign sense) structures capable of explaining all behavioural phenomena. And since he was unable, in the case of genuine language and thought, to conceive of a physical structure capable of doing the job, he was led to posit a non-physical entity – the rational soul – to perform these functions. His conclusions, given the current state of science in his time, were entirely reasonable.

Whether it has genuine explanatory power is another question. The phenomena of creativity, innovativeness and freedom from determination by specific stimuli all being, according to Descartes, inexplicable on mechanical and physical principles, are supposedly explained by positing something *non*-mechanical and *non*-physical. But that still leaves us in the dark (one might object) as to *how* exactly this 'rational soul' is able to do the job that a physical structure cannot do. It is this kind of worry that leads many modern naturalism philosophers to reject any immaterialist view of the mind as 'spooky' – that is to say, mysterious and lacking any real explanatory bite. The defender of Descartes's position might reply that his arguments about language and thought nevertheless demonstrate the limits of naturalism: there are certain characteristic human abilities and performances that cannot be accounted for as the outputs of a 'closed' physical system. The philosophical issues involved here are intricate and fascinating, and the debate which Descartes started will surely continue for a very long while.

THE EMOTIONS AND THE GOOD LIFE

When a dog sees a partridge it is naturally disposed to run towards it; and when it hears a gun fired, the noise naturally impels it to run away. Nevertheless, setters are commonly trained so that the sight of a partridge makes them stop, and the noise they hear afterwards, when someone fires at the bird, makes them run towards it. These things are worth noting in order to encourage each of us to make a point of controlling our passions. For since we are able, with a little effort, to change the movements of the brain in animals devoid of reason, it is evident that we can do so still more effectively in the case of human beings. Even those who have the weakest souls could acquire absolute mastery over all their passions, if we employed sufficient ingenuity in training and guiding them.

Passions of the Soul [Les passions de l'âme, *1649*], Part I, article 50
(AT XI 370: CSM I 348)

The objects which strike our senses move parts of our brain by means of the nerves, and there make as it were folds, which undo themselves when the object ceases to operate; but afterwards the place where they were made has a tendency to be folded again in the same manner by another object resembling even incompletely the original object. For instance, when I was a child I loved a little girl of my own age who had a slight squint. The impression made by sight in my brain when I looked at her cross-eyes became so closely connected to the simultaneous impression which aroused in me the passion of love, that for a long time afterwards when I saw persons with a squint I felt a special inclination to love them simply because they had that defect. At that time I did not know that was the reason for my love; and indeed as soon as I reflected on it and recognized that it was a defect, I was no longer affected by it. So, when we are inclined to love someone without knowing the reason, we may believe that this is because he has some similarity to something in an earlier object of our love, though we may not be able to identify it.

Letter to Chanut, 6 June 1647 (AT V 57: CSMK 322)

I make a distinction between the love which is purely intellectual or rational and the love which is a passion. The first, in my view, consists simply in the fact that when our soul perceives some present or absent good, which it judges to be fitting for itself, it joins itself to it willingly, that is to say, it considers itself and the good in question as forming two parts of a single whole. Then, if on the one hand the good is present – that is, if the soul possesses it, or is possessed by it, or is joined to it not only by its will but also in fact and reality in the appropriate manner – in that case, the movement of the will which accompanies the knowledge that this is good for it, is joy; if on the other hand the good is absent, then the movement of the will which accompanies the knowledge of its lack is sadness; while the movement which accompanies the knowledge that it would be a good thing to acquire it is desire. All these movements of the will which constitute love, joy, sadness, and desire, in so far as they are rational thoughts and not passions, could exist in our soul even if it had no body. For instance, if the soul perceived that there are many very fine things to be known about nature, its will would be infallibly impelled to love the knowledge of those things, that is, to consider it as belonging to itself. And if it was aware of having that knowledge, it would have joy; if it observed that it lacked the knowledge, it would have sadness; and if it thought it would be a good thing to acquire it, it would have desire. There is nothing in all these movements of its will which would be obscure to it, nor anything of which it could fail to be perfectly aware, provided it reflected on its own thoughts. But while our soul is joined to the body, this rational love is commonly accompanied by the other kind of love, which can be called sensual or sensuous. This . . . is nothing but a confused thought, aroused in the soul by some motion of the nerves, which makes it disposed to have the other, clearer, thought which constitutes rational love. Just as in thirst the sensation of the dryness of the throat is a confused thought which disposes the soul to desire to drink, but is not identical with that desire; so, in love a mysterious heat is felt around the heart, and a great abundance of blood in the lungs, which makes us open our arms as if to embrace something, and this inclines the soul to join to itself willingly the object presented to it.

Letter to Chanut, 1 February 1647 (AT IV 601–3: CSMK 306–7)

Descartes conceived of his philosophy as having important practical implications for human life. In these final extracts we see Descartes utilizing the results of his scientific research in physiology and psychology to construct a solution to the age-old problem of human weakness. Philosophers from Plato to the present day have been perplexed by how often our human pursuit of a worthwhile life can be blown off course by the unruly nature of our passions: often the impulses arising from our physical nature seem to pull us in the opposite direction to what reason dictates. In tackling this problem, Descartes offers some revolutionary suggestions for the re-training of the passions, based on an early version of stimulus–response theory.

In the first extract, from his last published work, *The Passions of the Soul* (*Les passions de l'âme*, 1649), Descartes adapts a point about animal training to the human sphere. In one of the earliest clear anticipations of what we now call the idea of a conditioned response, he offers a suggestion as to how the innately predetermined mechanisms of the body can be modified to our advantage. The idea that the good life requires training and habituation was not in itself new. Many centuries earlier, Aristotle had proposed that virtue depends on our having acquired the right habits of feeling and action, on our possession not just of 'right reason', but of the appropriate kinds of ingrained dispositions to feel and behave in the right ways. What Descartes now adds to this story is the perspective of the behavioural and physiological scientist who is able to investigate the physical causes of our emotional patterns of response, and in time learn to manipulate and 'reprogramme' them.

The second extract contains a striking example of this from Descartes's own experience – his propensity, due to a childhood experience, to be attracted to cross-eyed women. Part of his approach is physiological: as a result of sensory stimulation, a 'fold' (or neural pathway, as we might now say) is set up in the brain which predisposes us to react in similar ways to future stimuli of a like kind. Descartes now proposes that investigating the circumstances of the original stimulus can enable us to 'stand back', as it were, from the causal nexus (in a way in which animals are unable to do), and consider the possibility of modifying our future responses.

Descartes is often said, sometimes accusingly, to have a view of the mind as something perfectly transparent to the subject – an assumption which, since Freud, we tend to think of as naïve and unwarranted. But in fact, as so often, Descartes's true position is far more subtle than the caricature – in this case the 'transparency' caricature – suggests. It is true, as we saw in discussing the Cogito, that Descartes's meditator does reach a direct and indubitable awareness of his thinking processes: I am directly aware that I am thinking, and therefore that I must exist, as long as I am thinking. And he goes on to define thought as 'everything that is within us in such a way that we are immediately aware of it' (AT VII 160: CSM II 113). But when it comes to the passions, as we see from our present extract, things are far from transparent. The 'cross-eyed girl' example is used by Descartes to develop a strikingly original insight which in many ways anticipates Freud: the causal genesis and subsequent occurrence of the passions is intimately linked to bodily events in ways which often make the force of the resultant emotion opaque to reason.

When we are in the grip of a potentially damaging passion, what so often threatens to overwhelm us is precisely the fact that something is happening to us whose basis, in our physiological make-up, and our past psychological history, we only dimly, if at all, understand. Realizing this offers for the first time the hope that humans may be able to achieve successful 'management' of the passions. 'As soon as I reflected on [the causes],' says Descartes about his infatuation with cross-eyed women, 'I ceased to be affected by it.'

The ancient Stoic writers had been much preoccupied with the dangers of the passions, but the strategies they had offered for coming to terms with them were very repressive. The Stoic idea was to *control* the passions, or, even better, to cultivate a state of mind where they simply did not occur: this was the ideal of *apatheia* – freedom from passion. Descartes's proposal is, in effect, that we should adopt a new kind of 'therapy' for the passions. In the preface to his *Passions of the Soul*, he announced that he was examining the passions *en physicien* – from the point of view of a natural scientist. Those investigations led Descartes to an awareness of the extent to which the power of the passions depends on factors below the threshold of consciousness.

Descartes, the very thinker who is so often glibly accused of having a naïve theory of the 'transparency of the mind', is actually telling us, in his work on the passions, that our emotional life as embodied creatures is far from immediately transparent to conscious awareness. A proper understanding of our human nature involves recognition of the extent to which we are not just angelic minds inhabiting bodily mechanisms, but creatures whose deepest feelings are intimately tied up with structures and events that are often concealed from direct consciousness. Descartes's work in *Passions of the Soul* aims to offer a new kind of ethics, which will come to terms with the essential opacity to the conscious mind of the operation of the passions.

Descartes links his new approach to the passions with an analysis of the way in which the structure of our emotional lives is influenced by the forgotten events and pre-rational experiences of early childhood. In our third extract Descartes makes an important distinction between 'purely intellectual or rational love' and 'the love which is a passion'. The former consists simply in the calm volition of the soul to 'join itself' to some rationally perceived good. This is the kind of love, presumably, that a pure intellectual being such as an angel might enjoy, and which human beings experience when they pursue, rationally and without disturbance, those goods which their reason adjudges worthy to be obtained. But things are very different when, as so often happens, we desire something in an emotionally charged way, when, as we say, we feel 'churned up' about someone or something. Here there are powerful patterns of bodily response which have been laid down in the past; these are linked to urgent yet often confused emotions which we experience without fully understanding their causes. In such cases, 'the rational thoughts involved are accompanied by the confused feelings of our childhood which remain joined to them'. As Descartes says later in the letter, a full explanation of the passions would involve delving back into our early lives, right back to our experiences at the breast at infancy, 'when we first came into the world'; 'it is this which makes the nature of love hard for us to understand' (AT IV 606: CSMK 308). Any sound ethics, Descartes is telling us, will involve getting behind the present structure of our emotions in order to recover the past pattern of events that, often unbeknown to us, charges them with significance.

Human beings are often subject to anger and depression

because they sense their lives are dominated by forces outside their control. Descartes's theory of the passions promises a cure for this, by offering us the hope of an informed understanding of the psycho-physiological causes of the passions. The hope here is that we can eventually achieve a kind of psychic harmony. To take Descartes's example of love, he is implicitly suggesting that the two kinds of love (rational and passionate) no longer need pull us in opposite directions, once we have managed, not to suppress, but to *understand* the latter.

The urgent need for such a reconciliation was underlined by Descartes in an earlier letter to Princess Elizabeth, written in 1645:

> Often passion makes us believe certain things to be much better and more desirable than they are; then, when we have taken much trouble to acquire them, and in the process lost the chance of possessing other more genuine goods, possession of them brings home to us their defects; and thence arise dissatisfaction, regret and remorse. And so the true function of reason is to examine the just value of all the goods whose acquisition seems to depend in some way on our conduct, so that we never fail to devote all our efforts to trying to secure those which are in fact the more desirable. (AT IV 284: CSMK 264)

This may sound at first quite rationalistic, as if Descartes is reverting to the old Stoic recipe of suppression and avoidance. But the more he thought about and discussed this issue, the more Descartes came to believe that the passions were not to be suppressed – that some of them were a positive good – indeed, the sole source of our greatest human joys. All that was needed was a correct (physiological and psychological) understanding of their causes, and, hence, of the means to modify them, where necessary, and to bring them into harmony with reason.

That the passions are not intrinsically evil is consistent with Descartes's general theory of human nature. The 'substantial union' of soul and body which constitutes a human being requires, for its survival and well-being, not just intellect and volition, but the whole range of sensory and affective states (for example, hunger, to tell us when we need food). That we feel a characteristic kind of discomfort when the stomach is empty and the blood sugar low has obvious survival value in impelling us to eat (and thus relieving the feeling of hunger); that I feel pain when I put my hand on a hot stove is clearly beneficial in encouraging me to avoid such dangerous stimuli in future. If the good life is to be a life for human beings, the passions are to be embraced, since their operation, in general terms, is intimately related to our human welfare.

The qualification 'in general terms' is crucial. Because of the relatively rigid way innate physiological mechanisms and environmentally conditioned responses operate, we may become locked into patterns of behaviour that turn out to be harmful. In Descartes's example he feels powerfully drawn to cross-eyed women irrespective of what other good or bad qualities they may have. The way to deal with such irrational impulses is not to suppress the passions, but rather to use the resources of science and experience to try to understand what has caused things to go wrong. Only then can we set about trying to reprogramme our responses so that the direction in which we are led by the passions corresponds to what our reason perceives as the best option. 'Persons whom the passions can move most deeply,' Descartes wrote in the concluding sentences of his last published work, 'are capable of enjoying the sweetest pleasures of this life.' The picture he leaves his readers with here at the end of *Passions of the Soul* is an encouraging one: 'It is true that they may also experience the most bitterness when they do not know how to put these passions to good use, and when fortune works against them. But the chief use of wisdom lies in teaching us to be masters of our passions and to control them with such skill that the evils which they cause are quite bearable, and even become a source of joy' (AT XI 488: CSM I 404).

In bringing our journey through these readings of Descartes to a close, it is perhaps appropriate to end on this note of harmony and optimism. So often Descartes is presented as the dualist who split off mind from body, and left us with a gloomy picture of humankind as ghostly creatures, alienated from their own physicality. Yet the ethics which he offered as one of the most valuable fruits of his philosophical system is in the final analysis inspired by a vision of integration, where intellectual understanding and human passion work in tandem to generate a worthwhile existence.

The resulting harmony has resonances not just on the practical level of how we should live, but on the more theoretical level of what it is to philosophize. Descartes's philosophy is multi-dimensioned, and his system aims to integrate many different domains of thought – scientific, metaphysical and ethical. For this reason alone, the Cartesian ideal of a unified philosophical system serves as a valuable counterweight to the fragmented and compartmentalized approach to philosophy that has become so characteristic of the modern academic discipline. Should the subject ever completely break up into a series of hermetically sealed specialisms, it would surely lose its very *raison d'être* – the struggle to see how the many different areas of human thought are related. Descartes, who never abandoned that struggle, amply deserves his place as one of the world's very greatest philosophers.

CHRONOLOGY

1596 Born at La Haye (now renamed 'Descartes') near Tours, on 11 March.

1607–15 Attends Jesuit college of La Flèche, in Anjou.

1616 Studies law at the University of Poitiers.

1619 Travels to Germany, and on 10 November has vision of new mathematical and scientific system.

1628 Composes *Rules for the Direction of our Native Intelligence*. Moves to Holland, which he makes his permanent home, though with frequent changes of address.

1629 Begins working on *The World* (*Le Monde*), a treatise on physics and cosmology.

1633 Condemnation of Galileo. Withdraws *The World* from publication.

1637 Publishes *Discourse on the Method* (anonymously), together with three scientific essays, *Optics*, *Meteorology*, and *Geometry*.

1641 *Meditations on First Philosophy*, with the *Objections* and *Replies* (criticisms of noted philosophers and theologians, and the author's responses).

1643 Begins long correspondence with Princess Elizabeth of Bohemia.

1644 *Principles of Philosophy* published.

1645 Birth of Descartes's natural daughter Francine; the child died of scarlet fever at the age of five.

1647 Begins work on *Description of the Human Body*.

1649 Goes to Sweden at invitation of Queen Christina. Publishes *Passions of the Soul*.

1650 Dies in Stockholm, 11 February.

SUGGESTIONS FOR FURTHER READING

Primary sources:

Adam C. and Tannery, P. (eds.), *Œuvres de Descartes*, 12 vols, rev. edn. Paris: Vrin/CNRS, 1964–76. The complete works in the original Latin or French. Referred to as '**AT**'.

Cottingham, J., Stoothoff, R. and Murdoch, D. (eds.), *The Philosophical Writings of Descartes,* vols I and II. Cambridge: Cambridge University Press, 1985. Referred to as '**CSM**'.

Cottingham, J., Stoothoff, R., Murdoch, D. and Kenny, A. (eds.), *The Philosophical Writings of Descartes,* vol. III, The Correspondence. Cambridge: Cambridge University Press, 1991. Referred to as '**CSMK**'.

Cottingham, J. (ed.), *Descartes, Meditations on First Philosophy, with Selections from the Objections and Replies*. Cambridge: Cambridge University Press, rev. ed. 1996. The pagination of text of the *Meditations* in this volume is identical with that in CSM II.

Collections of essays

Cottingham, J. (ed.), *The Cambridge Companion to Descartes*. Cambridge: Cambridge University Press, 1992.

Cottingham, J. (ed.), *Reason, Will, and Sensation: Studies in Descartes's Metaphysics*. Oxford: Clarendon, 1994.

Cottingham, J. (ed.), *Descartes. Oxford Readings in Philosophy Series*. Oxford: Oxford University Press, 1998.

Doney, W. (ed.), *Descartes: A Collection of Critical Essays*. Garden City, NY: Doubleday, 1967.

Hooker, M. (ed.), *Descartes: Critical and Interpretive Essays*. Baltimore: Johns Hopkins University Press, 1978.

Moyal, G., *Descartes: Critical Assessments*, 4 vols. New York: Routledge, 1991.

Rorty, A. O. (ed.), *Essays on Descartes' Meditations*. Berkeley: University of California Press, 1986.

Voss, S. (ed.), *Essays on the Philosophy and Science of René Descartes*. Oxford: Oxford University Press, 1992.

General Books on Descartes's Philosophy

Cottingham, J., *Descartes*. Oxford: Blackwell, 1986.

Cottingham, J., *The Rationalists*. Oxford: Oxford University Press, 1988.

Cottingham, J., *A Descartes Dictionary*. Oxford: Blackwell, 1993.

Gaukroger, S., *Descartes: An Intellectual Biography*. Oxford: Clarendon, 1995.

Grene, M., *Descartes*. Brighton: Harvester, 1985.

Kenny, A., *Descartes*. New York: Random House, 1968.

Loeb, L., *From Descartes to Hume: Continental Metaphysics and the Development of Modern Philosophy*. Ithaca, NY: Cornell University Press, 1981.

Rodis-Lewis, G., *Descartes*. Paris: Libraire Générale Française, 1984.

Smith, N. Kemp, *New Studies in the Philosophy of Descartes*, London: Macmillan, 1966.

Williams, B., *Descartes: The Project of Pure Enquiry*. Harmondsworth: Penguin, 1978.

Wilson, M. D., *Descartes*. London: Routledge, 1966.

Other studies

Clarke, D., *Descartes' Philosophy of Science*. Manchester: Manchester University Press, 1982.

Cottingham, J., A Brute to the Brutes? Descartes' Treatment of Animals. In *René Descartes, Critical Assessments,* ed. G. Moyal. London: Routledge, 1991, vol. IV; and in *Descartes. Oxford Readings in Philosophy Series*, ed. J. Cottingham.

Cottingham, J., *Philosophy and the Good Life: Reason and the Passions in Greek, Cartesian and Psychoanalytic Ethics*. Cambridge: Cambridge University Press, 1997, Ch. 3.

Doney, W. (ed.), *Eternal Truths and the Cartesian Circle*. New York: Garland, 1987.

Frankfurt, H.G., *Demons, Dreamers and Madmen*. Indianapolis: Bobbs Merrill, 1970.

Garber, D., *Descartes' Metaphysical Physics*. Chicago: University of Chicago Press, 1992.

Gaukroger, S., *Cartesian Logic*. Oxford: Clarendon, 1989.

Hintikka, J. Cogito ergo sum: Inference or Performance. In *Eternal Truths and the Cartesian Circle*, ed. W. Doney. New York: Garland, 1987.

John Paul II, *Memory and Identity*. London: Orion, 2005.

Jolley, N., *The Light of the Soul: Theories of Ideas in Leibniz, Malebranche and Descartes*. Oxford: Oxford University Press, 1990.

Markie, P., *Descartes's Gambit*. Ithaca, NY: Cornell University Press, 1986.

Menn, S., *Descartes and Augustine*. Cambridge: Cambridge University Press, 1998.

Putnam, H., The Nature of Mental States. In *Mind, Language and Reality: Philosophical Papers*, vol. II. Cambridge: Cambridge University Press, 1975.

Ryle, G., *The Concept of Mind*. London: Hutchinson, 1949.

Shea, W.M., *The Magic of Numbers in Motion: The Scientific Career of René Descartes*. Canton, MA: Science History Publications, 1991.

INDEX

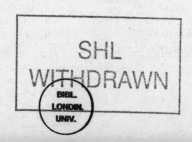